THE REJECTION THAT CHANGED MY LIFE

ALSO BY JESSICA BACAL

Mistakes I Made at Work:
25 Influential Women Reflect on What They Got
Out of Getting It Wrong

THE

REJECTION
THAT CHANGED
MY LIFE

25+ Powerful Women on Being
Let Down, Turning It Around, and
Burning It Up at Work

JESSICA BACAL

PLUME

PLUME

An imprint of Penguin Random House LLC
penguinrandomhouse.com

LIBRARY OF CONGRESS CATALOGING-IN-PUBLICATION DATA
has been applied for.

ISBN 9780593187654 (paperback)
ISBN 9780593187661 (ebook)

Printed in the United States of America
1   3   5   7   9   10   8   6   4   2

For my parents

Contents

THE REJECTION THAT
CHANGED MY LIFE

INTRODUCTION

What made me think people would be willing to tell me about their rejections?

Yes, I'd edited an earlier book, *Mistakes I Made at Work,* in which I'd asked women to talk about work mistakes, but that seemed somehow less threatening than asking about rejections. At Smith College, where I direct the Narratives Project, my ambitious students heard a lot of gratifying yeses about fellowships, internships, and jobs—but also some disappointing nos. They trashed or deleted these rejections; they'd never seemed too interested in *publishing* them.

Maybe I was setting myself up for failure. One potential interviewee, a successful businesswoman, balked: "Does *rejection* have to be in the title?" A friend in the media e-mailed that certainly she had learned from her rejections but wasn't comfortable sharing. "I'm sorry!!!!" she added. Many of my invitations to participate in this book went unanswered. A professor I deeply respect e-mailed saying she didn't want her story in the book: "Honestly," she wrote, "I'm not sure what the point is."

The point is this: Reading stories like these make people feel they aren't alone. I'd heard from readers that they'd reached for *Mistakes I Made at Work* after tough workdays, and it had comforted them. We live with the myth that our careers should be linear, that messing up is like landing on the wrong spot in Chutes and Ladders: one god-awful day and we'll be sent plunging downward. In reality, our career paths can zigzag and bump along—it doesn't mean we've gone down a chute.

Still, a rejection can feel like that. In fact, the more I thought about it, the more I realized that I personally had often tried hard to avoid rejection.

During my senior year of high school, I applied early to college, ostensibly because I liked the school—but also because it meant that if I got in, I could take back all my other applications. I was accepted and went to Carleton in Minnesota; it's a wonderful place, but applying early decision meant I never had to learn whether I would be accepted (or rejected) at the other schools.

Even within the last ten years, I applied to two doctoral programs and was somewhat shocked and embarrassed to be rejected by *both*. I'd overreached, I thought. I wasn't as smart as I'd imagined. My first choice had been the University of Pennsylvania, but I convinced myself that it would have been a terrible idea anyway, since it meant I'd have to leave my family every month. Then one day over lunch, my friend Julio at Smith said, "People get rejected from these programs all the time! Just reapply!" I realized that if I were talking to a student, that was the advice I would give: Don't take a first rejection as an absolute. Why couldn't I give that advice to myself? I decided to try again and was thrilled when I was admitted. (The time away from my family *was* hard, but I earned my doctorate.)

Curiously, I never avoided romantic rejection. I had no problem asking people on dates. At age twenty-eight, I pursued my now husband with a mix tape that featured my favorite Bruce Springsteen songs. It was school and work that somehow made me feel vulnerable. I didn't want to hear that I wasn't good enough. Rejection would confirm something I already knew about myself: that I actually wasn't smart enough or accomplished enough and didn't belong in those spaces anyway.

Rejection can reinforce a message that many of us are receiving all the time in small ways: You don't belong. Raina Brands and Isabel Fernandez-Mateo, researchers at London Business School, have shown that female executives are less likely than their male peers to reapply for jobs in leadership after being turned down. It's *not* because women are less resilient or persistent, but because they have already experienced years of small rejections in work cultures that generally value maleness more. They have felt a lack of belonging that leads them to believe it would be foolish to reapply. For women of color, rejection at work is compounded by racism. Highly qualified women of color are less likely than white women to get credit for their accomplishments; a major report from McKinsey and LeanIn.org showed that women of color get less support than white and male peers do from their supervisors.

And let's face it—a big part of why I avoided rejection for so long is because it sucks. It just feels bad. But in this case, with this book, it was more personal than ever. I had just experienced a major rejection (more on that later), and it made me think that it was time to get some support and gather a book-length collection of virtual mentors. I wanted them for myself, for my undergraduates at Smith College, and for readers. I imagined I would find professionals from diverse backgrounds who could remind us of how common rejection is and how it truly isn't the end of the world—sometimes it's the beginning.

I knew from my work as director of the Narratives Project that sharing personal stories was powerful and even transformative. And I'd seen after publishing my first book, *Mistakes I Made at Work*, that it was useful to normalize the uncomfortable and crappy parts of work, to hear "This happened to me. It sucked. You will get through it."

That book included only interviews with women; this one does too, even though I think about gender differently than I did in 2014, when *Mistakes* was published. I understand now that the categories of "male" and "female" feel way too restrictive for many people. And social science overwhelmingly shows that men and women aren't that different—in fact, we are "basically alike in terms of personality, cognitive ability and leadership," according to the American Psychological Association.

But there was something about pairing "rejection" and "women" that I found especially intriguing. We live in a culture where "masculine" shouts strength and independence, while "feminine" whispers softness and collaboration. It puts both sexes in a bind, but at work, it hurts women more. Women are not supposed to be self-promoting or *too* assertive or angry. We're supposed to look for the point of connection, for approval. So I wanted to hear about what happened to women when they hadn't gotten it, when they had been outright rejected.

Plus, when I thought of my own experiences of rejection, it was other women's stories that had helped me. I was inspired by women I knew, like Dr. Elizabeth Bell (interviewed in this book), who was rejected from medical school when she first applied. I was awed by my friend Heather Abel, who dealt with a lot of rejection before her beautiful novel was published to glowing reviews. I was inspired by the women who participated in my last book, like Judith Warner, who lost a journalism job she loved, found meaning in writing about mental health, and was deeply gratified by the people who said her work helped them. These were the kinds of stories that I wanted to hear.

I wanted them because of my own recent, and very memorable, experience with a work rejection. Even when you are generally a rejection avoider, sometimes you are drawn to making yourself vulnerable. In 2019, I was working at Smith and loved my job, but I applied for a different job at the college. This meant writing a kick-ass, three-page cover letter with my vision for a new center, giving a presentation—which I practiced for hours in front of friends—and asking colleagues for letters of reference. It meant being interviewed by people who already knew me; after years of informal, friendly interactions, we now sat formally and somewhat awkwardly around a conference table so they could assess my potential.

After the application process was over, I checked my e-mail obsessively; I privately observed and interpreted the facial expressions of colleagues. When we passed each other on the street, did that friendly smile reveal a sense of confidence in my abilities— or was it sympathy?

The head of the hiring committee was actually my supervisor, a woman who is brilliant, elegant, and kind. Several weeks after I applied, she called me into her office and closed the door. When she told me, "We've offered the job to someone else," I made an effort to sit in an open-armed, relaxed way (*I'm not upset*) but with good posture (*I still feel good about myself*). She was clearly worried about my feelings, and I didn't want to make the conversation harder; I also hated the idea of her wondering if I might cry.

"Okay," I said.

"I told the team," said my supervisor, "and they were all worried, asking if you'd be okay. I told them you would."

"I am," I said. "I really am fine." (*They think I'm pathetic.*) I wondered who *had* gotten the job—like, really, there was someone better than *I was*!? But I also felt the flutter of something else. If I wasn't given the job, it meant I didn't have to *do* the job. That sense of relief was important data. Maybe I didn't want the job at all.

It turned out that the worst part of not getting the job came afterward: I e-mailed the people who had written letters of reference, feeling like I'd let them down. I walked around campus and wondered: *Does she know? Does he?* It was humbling, but being humbled is not a bad thing. It's kind of stunning to say aloud, but I'd gotten so many things I wanted in my life. I hadn't gotten this. My inner voice (mean version) murmured, *You spoiled brat. Big deal! How many people* never *get what they want?* My inner voice (nice, normal version) responded, *It feels bad, and it's okay to feel bad—but, yes, do keep some perspective about how lucky your life has been.*

And even though the rejection was hard, my supervisor showed me that it wasn't a blanket statement about my worth to her or to Smith. She gave me the chance to develop and teach a for-credit class at Smith and invited me to join a new team, which included the woman hired to run the center (the job I didn't get).

Turns out, yeah, she actually *is* really good at creating something new. She is kicking ass and I'm learning a lot from her.

But back to my relief at not getting the job. That relief was important to notice. In doing interviews for this book, I learned that it's possible, after the initial bad feelings, to separate yourself from a rejection and use your reaction to it as data about your future path.

Talking to the wonderful women who contributed to this book, I was amazed to learn about how much *practice* many successful people have in dealing with rejection. Singers, social scientists, and comedians all talked about the systematic ways in which they collected rejections—sometimes on purpose—and just kept going.

I also heard about significant ways in which many women's lives were changed and improved after being dealt a blow. People have written about this phenomenon in various ways throughout history; psychologists call it "post-traumatic growth," the transformation that can happen after a personal crisis. "Post-traumatic growth" is also a term that can be used for nations and whole societies. As I write this in April 2020, the world is in a time of upheaval. But there are signs of growth and strength—in the United States, more women are leading in Congress than ever before. As one of my interviewees, Pamela Shifman, told me, "It feels like we're in a moment when women's power is unprecedented."

I kept going on this book even as the rejections (from people who didn't want to talk about rejection) rolled in. My first inkling that *maybe* readers would be interested came at the doctor's office. I was there with a bad cold, and the doctor asked if her intern could do my intake.

The intern was a woman in her twenties who had such positive and calming energy, you just knew she would make a great doctor. When she asked if I'd been under stress and I responded, "Some," she asked why.

"Well," I said, "I work full time, I have two children and two dogs, and I'm writing a book."

"Oh!" she said, looking up from the computer where she was logging my symptoms. "What's it about?"

"Rejection at work," I told her. The intern broke into a huge smile. There was a knock at the door and the doctor came in; the intern turned to her: "She's writing a book!" The doctor was less interested. But when my visit was over (I was fine), the intern turned to me. "I can't wait to read it," she said, then slipped out of the room.

I felt a spark of excitement. The readers! They would be out there, I hoped. I wanted them to find comfort in this book, to feel supported by a band of women who had all been there. I wanted to remind them that there is power in sharing our stories. I wanted to show the ways in which rejection can make each of us stronger.

At the back, readers will find a workbook, with exercises linked to some of the social science related to rejection. The goal of these is to help you access the power of your own story.

PART 1

Rejection Is Data

I'd been developing programs at Smith to help students find meaning and purpose, and those programs were increasingly valuable. I was feeling pretty good, until an idea began to circulate that we should consider bringing in a group called Project Wayfinder, which had developed a curriculum . . . to help college students find meaning and purpose. The idea was that they might be part of a larger set of professional development workshops for faculty and staff. They were from *Stanford*.

On the day I learned this, the idea made me feel so depressed that it was almost like a weight was pushing me down. I walked out of a meeting into a perfect New England spring day and decided to decompress by going home for lunch. Then I took my dogs for a short walk; lilac trees were in bloom, and there was a light breeze. Walking, I remembered that my work with college students was meaningful to me and gave me purpose. I needed to just let go of my ego.

Eventually (in all truth, several months later) I calmed down about Stanford and took a look at the Wayfinder curriculum. It was beautiful; there were overlaps with what I did, but some stuff was better. That feeling of rejection was data about myself: I can get competitive, and also defensive. Noted—I'd be ready and re-member both next time, and I would remind myself to take a deep breath and stay receptive.

It can be useful to see the experience of rejection, including our own reactions to it, as just data. It may take time and likely won't happen right away, but it's a great way of giving ourselves a little space.

I loved the job I already had, and over the next couple of months, I became invested in new creative projects at Smith. When a senior from China asked me to guide international students in making digital stories about their lives, I was thrilled. My supervisor asked me to start developing a course called Designing Your Path that would help students figure out where they'd been and where they wanted to go. Both of these were exciting projects and reminded me that I had a lot to offer.

Mine is a pretty positive rejection-as-data story. But we also need to look at the flipside of rejection as data. While the information we glean from a perceived or actual rejection can be use-ful, it can also be demoralizing, especially when we intuit that bias is at play.

In one story in the upcoming section, law professor Joan Wil-liams talks about turning down burdensome extra work on her university's admissions committee, only to be seen as "not a team player." Another interviewee, Isa Watson, got a performance re-view that gave her low marks in "analytics," which has to do with using data to make decisions—but Watson had a PhD in chem-istry and was quite comfortable using data. When she asked how she might improve, no one could tell her. Laura Weidman Pow-ers, a Harvard and Stanford graduate, moved to a new city and needed a job. She heard "no"—or just crickets—after every application.

These women didn't initially see their own rejections as examples of bias. They saw what was right in front of them, their own singular story, and felt rejection and hurt. But Williams *did* notice that her university assigned only women to the admissions committee. Watson was a rising star in investment banking but was also black in a white-dominated environment. Weidman Powers was a black woman looking for work in white, male-dominated Silicon Valley. Gradually, these women moved into positions of power themselves, but their stories are reminders that rejection can be data that's less about you and more about the system in which you're operating. While that can be painful, it can be part of the big picture that informs your next steps.

ANGELA DUCKWORTH

Rejection is hard for me, even though I study it. I'm not the kind of person who's just like, "Oh, I love critical feedback; telling me what I did wrong is like whipped cream." It's really not. It's like a sour lemon.

Angela Duckworth is one of the most successful psychologists of our generation. She is famous for developing the theoretical framework around "grit": the combination of passion and perseverance for a long-term goal.

When I spoke with Duckworth over the phone, I learned she also has a good sense of humor. We had arranged the interview through Duckworth's assistant, Jamie, who had written polite, friendly e-mails like "Happy to help find a time for you and Angela to talk!" and "Let me check in with Angela and I'll get back to you as soon as I can."

When we finally got on the phone, I let Duckworth know that I appreciated her assistant setting up our conversation. "I don't know if Jamie told you," I said, "but you and I have a mutual friend, Andy Sokatch."

"Yes! Andy is such a good guy." Duckworth laughed. "But I have to tell you, Jamie is a robot. A very smart robot." I had been e-mailing back and forth with her virtual assistant as if it was a person.

Duckworth is on the faculty at the University of Pennsylvania, and she co-founded Character Lab, which uses psychological science to help children thrive. She studies grit and self-control, which she says are not the same—more like first cousins. Self-control is the ability to resist fun temptations in the moment in order to do something *less fun* but good for you—even ten minutes later. Grit is about the ability to work toward goals you really care about that are further out.

In 2013, she received a MacArthur Fellowship—the prize often known as the MacArthur Genius Grant—a large sum of no-strings-attached funding given to the recipient out of the blue. Duckworth may be the first Genius Grant recipient I have ever spoken to, and she was extremely down-to-earth and open.

Lessons I've Learned

When you tell someone a new idea, you are looking for approval—we all are. But that doesn't always mean you need it in order to move forward.

One of my early research projects in graduate school examined middle schoolers and self-control. I was familiar with "the marshmallow test," and you may be too: A researcher in the 1980s would put a marshmallow in front of a preschooler and tell the child that she'd be right back. The researcher would mention that if the child could wait and *not* eat the marshmallow, then the prize would be two marshmallows when she returned. The children who waited turned out to have more self-control than peers across multiple non-marshmallow contexts, such as at school.

I wanted to test self-control in middle schoolers, so I wondered: What's the marshmallow test for older kids? Early piloting told me that it would not be something that I could do easily. Middle schoolers didn't want toys; they didn't care about snacks. They were not about to get all excited about an Oreo. Plus, the school administrators were not thrilled about food as a reward. They were like, "You don't know who is going to be allergic to it, and we don't want to be liable." I wondered, "What is something that everybody wants at some level?" It didn't take long to realize that the teenagers in my studies would all appreciate a little pocket money.

I took this idea to my doctoral advisor. "I'm going to do this thing where I give kids a dollar," I told him. "Then I'm going to see if they want to keep the dollar—or give it back and in a week get *two* dollars. And that choice is going to be a measure of their self-control."

Right away, my advisor said, "That's a terrible idea." He began trying to poke holes in the plan, asking, for example, "How will the students know you'll come back?"

I was disappointed not to have his approval. There I sat, a newbie graduate student, and the person whose advice I most respected was telling me not to go ahead with my experiment. I had to question whose judgment was better—my own or that of this super-famous person who had been doing psychology for forty-five years?

And maybe that's the difference between backing down and

moving forward. How firm are your convictions? In my case, I thought it *was* a good experiment. The fact that he didn't think so actually motivated me. Plus, I didn't have a better idea. I decided to go with my judgment. I told him, "Even though you think it's a bad plan, I'm doing it anyway."

As a side note, at my twenty-fifth college reunion I asked one of my good friends, Tina, "Just candidly between you and me, I'm interested in what you think. I'm not the smartest one here; I'm not the prettiest. I'm not the richest or most athletic one here. Why do you think I've had the success that I have had?"

She replied, "You're not afraid."

I think that's true. I wasn't afraid for the experiment to not work out. What was the worst that was going to happen? I would blow a few hundred dollars. It wasn't the end of the world.

My advisor had been right about this experiment in that there *were* logistical issues to fix: Whereas the marshmallow test takes an hour to do each person, one-on-one, I wanted to be able to give the test to a whole classroom. Also, I was going to give the kids money, but I didn't want them to walk around knowing *other* kids' choices, whether they had kept one dollar or waited for two. I gave each kid an envelope, saying, "This has your name on it. Take out the dollar bill *or* put it back and you can have two dollars later." I had *all* of them pass back the envelopes, whether they took the dollar bill out or not.

My test ended up being essential to part of the measurement battery for self-control in middle schoolers, and in fact it predicted kids' grades as well as their IQ scores. I wrote up the experiment and submitted it to what is arguably the most prestigious journal in my field. It was accepted, and when my advisor found out, he was very proud of me.

What my early publication success meant, in part, was that I didn't know for a long time just how hard it is to get published. You get rejected most of the time, and it's a hard rejection, with reader comments to the effect of "Let me tell you all the reasons you are stupid and boring and this is unbelievable and somebody already did this." But I didn't know that. When I submitted my article, I received gentle peer reviews, like "It's pretty good, maybe you could change this one little thing?" Then it was published.

Sometimes I wonder whether early success is important to maintaining that beginner's drive. If I had received harsh criticism early in my career, I might not have proceeded with the same level of energy and enthusiasm. I think that with kids and people starting out, having some early wins helps to develop confidence.

I'm very open with my graduate students. I try not only to share with them my own failures, but also to correct the wrong ideas that they and others have about success. When you're starting out in academia and get rejected, you feel like an idiot. And you might look around and pay attention to someone else's successes. But failures are hidden. People don't put their failures and their errors into the public realm, so we walk around thinking that we're the only ones feeling insecure.

I try to read articles about things like that. Most recently, I read and sent around a study of academics who *almost* got a particular grant but didn't get it. So they were probably about as deserving of funding but didn't get it. The study examined what happened to them, and by some metrics, they ended up being more productive than their peers!

If you get defensive when people tell you things that you could do better, you're human. It's important to give ourselves a break.

There are times when people are rejected and it redoubles their motivation. I tend to have that response. When the MacArthur Foundation said they were giving away 100 million dollars a few years ago, I didn't really have much interest in it. Then a colleague said, "Oh, you'll never get it," and I was like, "Oh, now I want it." There was a kind of "I'll show *you*!" response, an underdog reaction that I recognize in myself and in others whom I study.

This particular MacArthur Fellowship was called the 100& Change. It was a 100-million-dollar grant given to researchers who aimed to solve "a critical problem of our time." In order to submit our project, Behavior Change for Good, we had to first compete within the University of Pennsylvania, which had something like fifty submissions from faculty. We were chosen out of dozens of professors in our university, but then we competed with applicants from other organizations in several more rounds. We had to make a video; we needed letters of support from every organization with whom we had worked. A couple of dozen world-class scientists from different universities around the world had to sign off, and so did their universities. This all meant a lot of time and effort. Of course, the idea itself also needed to be refined. Overall, applying for the MacArthur Fellowship was hours and hours of work every month before we finally submitted it.

My co-applicant was my colleague Katy Milkman, and we are like sisters. We love each other; we like each other. We fight with each other. I wear her sweaters; she wears mine. One day, after we had submitted the fellowship application and it had been sent on by our university, Katy called me. I was traveling for work, and I remember I was in the hotel gym, standing beside a weight rack.

"They didn't pick us," she said.

At first I thought I wasn't hearing her correctly; the gym was noisy. I asked, "What did you say?"

And she repeated, "They didn't pick us." Katy explained that there were still two hundred projects in the running, but we had been eliminated.

I was upset, but also—and this is not especially flattering—I was sort of surprised. I was like, "What?"

We were both devastated, partly because we had put in so much effort. Sometimes people are afraid to try because the harder you try, the harder you fall. And we had *really* tried.

When I think about grit, it isn't about being able to blow off a rejection or failure *in the moment;* it isn't about not crying. You can cry all you want. The question is, do you get up again? And we did. After we'd cried a little bit, we asked ourselves, how do we proceed? We were still doing the project we had submitted, because it was a good idea. We would just have a lot less money.

The feedback that we got from the MacArthur Foundation was actually useful. They said, "It's too early. There doesn't seem to be a high enough probability that you could solve the problem you're putting on the table." We actually thought that was good feedback. Maybe they were looking for a lower-risk grantee, and maybe that was a good thing. The proposal that won was submitted by Sesame Workshop and the International Rescue Committee, and their project aimed to educate refugee children in the Middle East—that is indeed a social problem of enormous significance.

When I get discouraged—which I honestly do; I get discouraged a lot—I remind myself that I'm in it for the long game. Sometimes I'm reminded of that by other people, like Katy or my husband. If you focus on one day, you can pack it up and go home. But you really do have to think of it as a long game. Not every day is going to be good.

People have different coping mechanisms; what I often do is called "support seeking" in psychology. When I have a problem, it's not long before a lot of people know about it. If things are not going well in my research, I whine about it to my husband, to my closest collaborators—and now they know about my problems, and they do what people do, which is to try to help me solve them. I know it varies for everyone, but in my case, my husband is a huge support. More tears have gone into his shirt collar than you can imagine.

I believe in resourcefulness and grit, but there is a lot of misunderstanding about grit. Just because humans are capable of overcoming adversity doesn't mean we shouldn't work as a society to change the ways in which adversity is meted out—to reduce inequality.

For all people, regardless of gender or origins, ideally life should be a series of experiences that are challenging in a way that is appropriate, not traumatic. People should be encountering things that they can almost do but that are not *easy*. At the same time, systemic support is so important. If we had equality of challenge and support, we wouldn't see these ridiculous gender imbalances at the top of many fields. I don't mean person-to-person support only; I mean structural supports, like parental leave policy, workday flexibility so people can take their kids or other family members to doctor's appointments, the ability to work from home if your kids are sick.

I've heard from so many women and individuals from underrepresented backgrounds who've reached the top of their fields and say that if you're at the top, you are sure as heck gritty because it was not an easy climb; there were many more obstacles in your way than there were for straight white men. I haven't looked into it myself, but it's a very reasonable proposition.

ANGELA DUCKWORTH'S TIPS

TIP 1—When you get rejected, you feel like you're the only one to whom this has happened—but that's not true. Failure happens to everyone. There is actually a name for this phenomenon: pluralistic ignorance. You assume something about everyone else, but that assumption is inaccurate.

TIP 2—Passions are developed, not discovered. It can take a long time—even years—for you to develop a love for a certain career. So don't quit a job too early just because it doesn't immediately feel like a "calling."

TIP 3—I'm a big believer in vulnerability—sharing with people you care about and getting support from one another.

ANDIE KRAMER

I don't think that a month goes by without some sort
of rejection. Do you view it as a rejection or as a learning experience? I really have worked hard to try to
view it as a learning experience.

I felt an instant connection to Andie Kramer when I learned she
and her husband have four cats and four dogs—I have two
dogs but would *ideally* have many more. She told me that she
would be hanging Christmas decorations as we talked, then proceeded to tell me about growing up in Chicago, where she still
lives. Kramer is a partner in a major international law firm and
leads its Financial Products, Trading and Derivatives Group.

I also appreciate Kramer because her most recent book, *It's Not
You, It's the Workplace,* tells readers—even if they've only read the
title—that her book is not about what women need to do better
or differently to adapt to a sexist work environment. She co-wrote
that book and her first book, *Breaking Through Bias,* with her
husband, Al Harris, also a lawyer.

"We need to enlist male allies," Kramer told me. She has found
that when she and her husband give talks about their books, au-
diences tend to hear things one way from her and another way
from him. "I've had experiences in which I know that if I said to

a group of men, 'You don't get this problem,' they would be roll-ing their eyes and I would have lost them. If my husband were to say exactly the same thing, they'd be hanging on every word."

Andie Kramer was named by *The National Law Journal* as one of the 50 Most Influential Women Lawyers in America for her "demonstrated power to change the legal landscape, shape public affairs, launch industries, and do big things," and she has won numerous other awards. Her law firm was recently named one of the top workplaces for female lawyers and receives recog-nition for its gender diversity efforts.

Lessons I've Learned

Sometimes a work-related heartbreak can inform your next steps in a useful way.

When I was in high school in Chicago, I told my parents that I wanted to be a lawyer. We were a working-class family and my parents knew only one lawyer, so they asked if he would take me to lunch and talk with me about his work. Over lunch, he proceeded to tell me all the reasons why I did not want to be a lawyer: No one liked lady lawyers; if I was a lady lawyer, I would never have friends; I would be isolated at work and wouldn't have anyone to talk to; I would never get married or have any children. Basically, I would live my life lonely and un-happy.

I ignored him completely. I had dreams of going to a fancy Ivy League school or to a women's college, but that was not in the cards, so I went to the University of Illinois and found that you can get a fabulous education in a huge state school. Then I went to law school at Northwestern and learned that I loved tax law—it was like solving a puzzle. Between my second and third year in law school, I found a summer job at a large firm and had a couple of important learning experiences about the culture of white-collar work environments.

One lesson came when I was asked to do a research project on tax issues related to airplanes. I went to the law firm's library and beat the hell out of it—but only found cases about boats. When I went back to the lawyer who'd given me the assignment, he asked why I hadn't gone to the county library. I said, "You mean I'm allowed to leave the building?" Where I'd grown up, you punched a clock. If you weren't at the facility, you weren't at work. I hadn't known that leaving the building to do research was an option.

Another lesson came after that summer was over. It was an accepted truth at the time when I graduated law school that if you didn't get a job offer from your summer internship, there was something wrong with you. I did expect an offer, because I'd gotten a lot of praise from lawyers I worked with at the big firm. Lawyers would write things like "You've obviously got this figured out" and other flattering comments on memos I turned in.

But when the summer was over, I got a phone call from the lawyer in charge of the firm's summer intern program. "I have really sad news," he said, "but I'm sorry—you don't have a job offer." I was shocked. The lawyers at his firm had praised my work so highly. Could he tell me why?

Apparently, one of the most senior lawyers had commented that Andie Kramer "would get a job over his dead body." I racked my brain. I'd only had a fifteen-minute project with this guy, so I couldn't understand it.

It actually took me a number of years to figure it all out: To begin that fifteen-minute project I'd been called into this guy's office by his assistant. It was the size of half a basketball court. He was sitting at his desk with his feet on it and his hands behind his head—the ultimate power pose. I had been told that I should always shake hands when I introduce myself to someone, so I went to shake his hand and introduce myself. I didn't know anything about etiquette at that time, but I now know that if a man is sitting at his desk and you walk over to shake his hand, it's impolite for him to stay seated. The guy had to stand up. In retrospect, that was my first "mistake"—accidentally challenging the power dynamic by making him stand.

Then he motioned for me to go sit in the corner of his office where he had a low couch. It looked like a dog bed. I was already discombobulated because I could tell something was off in our interaction, but I didn't know what it was. He had two guest chairs on the other side of his desk, so I sat in one of those. He gave me my task, which was to incorporate some not-for-profit organization. It was like a ten-minute job. Then I left.

Apparently, I had acted too forthrightly by shaking his hand and making him get out of his chair; I had then been uppity by refusing a seat on his office dog bed. But I only realized these things later, looking back. When I learned I hadn't gotten the job, I worried I'd never get any job at all. There I was, with fabulous grades and great dreams that I would be this important lawyer. I was heartbroken.

But that heartbreak informed my next steps. I ended up getting an offer from another large and prestigious international firm in Chicago. I was sure I was going to join that firm. Then a law school classmate, probably one of the smartest people in my class, was clerking at a new firm that needed a tax lawyer. She encouraged me to go talk to them, and as a courtesy, I went.

It was a small firm and I immediately liked and connected with everyone there. They said, "We don't have a tax department, and we need one. Come work with us and we'll give you whatever additional training you want."

Having had such a horrible experience in the wake of my summer internship at that big firm, I decided that a small, friendly firm was the way to go. What could have been the worst work rejection of my life led to my being a little more proactive in finding the right fit, starting my career in a place that supported me completely, even though I was a woman. I didn't know it at the time, but that was unusual.

Each of us has many characteristics; learning to navigate workplace sexism doesn't necessarily mean that you're not being "authentic."

At a certain point, I had clients who needed the power that only a bigger law firm could offer. I moved over to a big firm, and that was when I became aware of gender bias. I served on our management committee and on our compensation committee, and I saw that women wrote their self-evaluations in this way: "I was on the ABC team, and I worked with so and so, and *we* saved the client half a billion dollars." The men who worked on that same project—even when they weren't project leaders—would self-evaluate this way: "*I* am a rock star: *I* climbed up to the top of the Empire State Building, found nineteen damsels in distress, and rescued them all. *I* single-handedly saved the client half a billion dollars." Who do you think was making more money? Men. That's what radicalized me. I started speaking and writing about what women needed to do in gender-biased workplaces to try to give themselves a fair shake.

In a big organization, what happens is that people assume that because you're a woman, you're going to show certain character-istics: You'll be communal, concerned for others, interested in col-laboration and in the well-being of the group. It's really all related to that terrible advice from my parents' friend who took me to lunch as a teenager. All through girlhood, we're trained to want to be liked, to be sweet and modest, expecting people to invite us to participate. The problem is that if we're strong and articulate and confident, it makes everybody's hair catch fire, women's and men's. Meanwhile, men are assumed to be more agentic, taking charge, pursuing their own success at all costs. And many of them do exactly that.

Unfortunately, if you could name three non-gender-biased workplaces and you were right, I would be shocked. Organiza-tions need to change. Men need to change. But if women work-ing today or starting our careers wait for organizations and men to do those things, we're going to be retired or dead or long gone from our careers. We have to push for institutional change while we navigate our own careers at the same time.

Studies show that women who use communal *or* agentic

characteristics as needed advance further in their careers than men do. In our book *Breaking Through Bias,* we coined the phrase "the Goldilocks Dilemma" for the double bind women face when they are only communal or agentic. Women are seen as too hard or soft but rarely just right. Women writing their own self-evaluations need to navigate the Goldilocks Dilemma. How can they take ownership of their accomplishments without coming off as too masculine? On a self-evaluation, a woman might say, "This year *I* designed the strategy that resulted in our client saving half a billion dollars. Here's how *I* did it." When her own performance is being evaluated, she doesn't hold back. If she has the data to prove it, then she's not going to get squashed.

Sometimes, when my co-author (my husband, Al) and I have talked about techniques to overcome gender bias, women respond, "I don't want to do those things. I want to be authentic." The reality is that authenticity doesn't mean that you're a cookie-cutter person. You have all sorts of communal and agentic characteristics that you can dip into. Authenticity is all about staying true to your values, not to one particular communication style.

ANDIE KRAMER'S TIPS

TIP 1—You don't have to be born with grit and resilience; they are things you can develop in order to deal with rejection, failures, and disappointments.

TIP 2—If you walk into the wall, fall down, and then try to walk through the same part of the wall again, you're just going to fall again. You've got to look around and say, "Is there a door? Is there some other way that I can get through here? What can I learn from hitting the wall?"

TIP 3—My mother died of brain cancer when she was sixty-three, and I remember the first couple of client crises that I handled after that when people around me were going nuts. I would reflect on the death of my mom and think, *It's only money. We're not doing brain surgery here.* I never would have said that out loud, but the reality is that we need to put things into perspective.

ISA WATSON

I always mentally reposition rejection by thinking,
"One rejection is one step closer to a yes."

I sa Watson was so much fun to talk to over the phone, it makes
sense that her company's mission is to connect people and
help them become friends. Watson is the CEO of Squad, a company that introduces individuals with similar interests, first online and then in real life.

Watson's effervescence belies her serious studiousness: In her
early twenties, she was publishing regularly in science journals as
she studied biochemistry at Cornell. Then she went to MIT. She
traveled all over the world as a high-level investment banker. But
a strong belief in the power of human connection—instilled from
her childhood—ultimately led her to see the need for Squad. In
telling me about the company, she said, "I'm black, you're white,
and I'm not that person who's like, 'I don't see color.' What I do
believe is that we have more in common than we realize."

When people join Squad, the app asks them questions about
the things that matter most, like "What's your top value right
now?" It then shows them four people they should meet at Squad-
curated events, like a panel or dinner series, and its algorithm
learns more about each person based on whom they connect
with. Watson says that the mission, in part, is to help people be

less lonely and to unplug. Since starting Squad, Isa Watson has been named one of the 30 Under 30 top entrepreneurs by *Inc.* magazine. She has been featured in *Forbes, Inc.,* and *Fast Company* and has been a guest on the *Today* show.

Lessons I've Learned

You don't have to accept a below-average performance review in an all-or-nothing way. You can work on critiques that resonate but call bullshit on the ones that don't.

I am from Saint Kitts and Nevis but spent most of my childhood in Chapel Hill, North Carolina. I was a brainy kid with intense, loving parents. That meant a lot of academic enrichment—physics one summer, mechanical engineering the next. I skipped a couple of grades and entered high school by age twelve. Around that time, we'd just gotten dial-up internet, and sometimes I would just sit at my parents' computer, researching drugs for illnesses like diabetes and heart disease, which had affected my family. When I learned about pharmaceutical companies, I clicked around to see who ran them: All their leadership teams were white men with business degrees. I decided then to study chemistry and become the CEO of a big pharma company so that I could help get treatments to people who needed them.

In college, I majored in chemistry and math at Hampton University, and then I got a master's degree in biochemistry at

Cornell. From there, I went on to MIT for an MBA. I had an excellent job offer from Merck, which makes pharmaceuticals, but another to work for the senior leadership team at JPMorgan Chase. Because I'd done a lot of lab work in my master's program, I thought working at an investment bank would be a great opportunity to get a different skill set.

JPMorgan was a big learning curve for me, partly because it was so different from a scientific research environment. In lab science, it's wrong to show up at the table without an opinion. If my boss suggested, "Why don't you try this solvent?" I could bluntly ask, "Why would that work?" Science communication is not about hierarchy; people are collaborative and direct.

At JPMorgan, everything was more oblique. I would get performance reviews that were hard to interpret; for example, a low rating in the category "ability to deal with ambiguity." One time, I got low marks on "analytics," but when I asked how to improve, no one could tell me. In science, when a professor or peer suggests that you're not thinking analytically enough, they literally mean, "You forgot to factor in something when you designed your experiment."

Luckily, I had a mentor in a woman named Carla Harris, who is vice chairman of Morgan Stanley. I'd print out my performance reviews and bring them to her for one-to-one meetings over breakfast at the MetLife building in Manhattan. Over egg-white omelets and tea, Carla would decode my reviews.

After reading the first one, she said, "Oh, they just don't like you. What did you do?"

I said, "I don't know."

Carla said, "I have a gut feeling that you're not being authentic at work, so they don't trust you."

Carla is a black woman who's had an extraordinarily successful career, and she is wonderful—I adore and respect her. But I had been told by other experienced black colleagues, "Listen, on Mondays when you're taking the subway to work, read up on how Tiger Woods is doing. See how the Yankees did. White people like golf and baseball, so walk in and start talking about that." I was a black woman working to fit into a mostly white office. I'm a very straightforward person, but I probably *wasn't* coming across as authentic—and people can read bullshit. After Carla told me that, I made a decision to just show up as me and to stop pretending I was interested in things I didn't care about. For example, I am a die-hard UNC Tar Heels basketball fan, so I talked about that—and people knew I was for real. They responded to me so much better.

Your work does not speak for itself.

Carla also told me, "Isa, you're not taking the time to learn your environment." She advised me to learn the players, to build relationships. I was very merit oriented, thinking, *My work speaks for itself.* But Carla told me, "Work doesn't speak," and she knew I would need these relationships in order to influence people.

I did start building relationships, using what Carla taught me and what I gleaned through my own reading and careful observation at work. I learned that people could act out when they felt insecure, and I made an effort to give credit to colleagues. I began rising through the ranks and accomplished a huge amount in the

New York and Hong Kong offices, including the development of a remote loan center that fulfilled 6 million dollars in business loans every year. I led another initiative for small businesses that, over time, brought in 1.2 billion dollars to the firm. But office politics played an increasingly large role as I was promoted to higher levels at the company. I had to navigate that, which was my least favorite part of the job, and frankly I also had to deal with white people's discomfort that a twenty-six-year-old black woman had so much power and authority.

Around the same time that I was becoming disenchanted with my job, something terrible happened in my family. My parents had, for many years, taken local high schoolers to visit colleges. My dad was the alumni president for his local chapter of Hampden-Sydney College; my parents personally paid for the trip each year. They were traveling by bus and it flipped, ejecting both my parents out the front window. My mom barely survived, and my dad did not survive.

It was completely devastating, and it made me think about everything that my parents had taught me. When I was growing up, they were always cultivating community. Our big house in North Carolina should have had a revolving front door because people were always coming in, always at our kitchen table. My dad used to say, "Isa, you're a blessed girl and it's your job to share your blessings with as many people as you can while you're on this planet." But I had never really understood. Now I started to realize the impact of human connection and community. People who hadn't seen my family for years told me, "Your parents changed the trajectory of my whole life."

I began to want to do something bigger. Even though I was in a highly visible role at JPMorgan as vice president of strategy, and even though there were amazing opportunities there, I wanted to do something that resonated with my spirit, that spoke to my purpose on the planet. I conceptualized the idea of Squad by thinking about gaps in online community building. We're in such a politically charged environment, so aware of our differences. I wanted to help people connect around similarities *in real life,* away from social media.

When I announced that I was leaving JPMorgan, several managing directors said, "Come work for me!" and it made me realize that I could always go back. Then, in order to replace me, they hired *two* men who were significantly more senior than I was. That was clear evidence that I had been producing, but it was time for something new.

Squad has raised more than 3.5 million dollars from investors who believe in its mission. I hear these stories about Squad meets between people from such different backgrounds: A thirty-seven-year-old Asian guy from Singapore, a thirty-two-year-old white woman from New York, and a twenty-five-year-old black guy from North Carolina. They had their Squad meet last weekend, and they vibed so hard. Now they regularly play basketball together. One is a dentist, and the other two are going to him for dental work. Stories like that make me feel like I'm honoring my parents through doing meaningful work. I'm also helping people to connect with one another in an authentic way.

ISA WATSON'S TIPS

TIP 1—Find a sponsor early. A sponsor is different from a mentor; while a mentor advises you, a sponsor is the person going to bat for you behind closed doors. Not having a sponsor at first slowed my ability to navigate the culture of JPMorgan Chase.

TIP 2—At JPMorgan Chase, there was a kind of emotional intelligence that I had to develop. I read *How to Win Friends and Influence People* like seven times, and I highly recommend it!

SARAH KOENIG

I talk to my kids about rejection and failure all the time: "Do you know how many jobs I had? You know how many things I didn't get? You know how many schools I didn't get into? Believe me, this is normal."

I first met Sarah Koenig when she was a member of an improv comedy group called Off-Off Campus at the University of Chicago. Onstage, Sarah was smart and energetic and hilarious. Nearly thirty years later, she was much the same during our interview. After college, she told me, she thought she would become an actress, but decided to get more serious and grown-up, which meant (in her mind) going to graduate school. She chose Russian literature, but only a couple of weeks in, she was sitting with fellow grad students at the Hungarian Pastry Shop—a Columbia University hangout—thinking, *I don't know who I am or what I'm doing.* She ended up deciding to leave, which was not "clean and easy" but "was like I was tortured. I felt like a failure. I felt like a fraud. I felt like a dummy. It was bad."

But quitting led to Sarah finding work that actually excited her. She spent more than a decade in journalism, landing at the public radio show *This American Life* and then moving on to create the first podcast to become a national phenomenon, *Serial,* which earned all the major broadcasting awards, including the duPont-Columbia, Scripps Howard, and Edward R. Murrow. It was the first podcast to win a prestigious Peabody Award. Essentially, *Serial* changed the way our culture understands podcasts, legitimizing the form with a technically superior production of narrative investigative journalism in podcast form.

Lessons I've Learned

Sending out job applications and hearing "no" constantly can make you feel like a failure, but it doesn't mean that you are *one.*

After college, I had a weird array of jobs, including a brief stint as a copy girl at the *Chicago Tribune*. I think they hired me because I was willing to work over Christmas. It was the olden times before computerized everything, and the way it worked was that each hour, an old white man would put his arm in the air and snap his fingers; then I would run and get the broadsheet news layout and deliver it to an editor's desk. That was my whole task, or I think it was. I never fully understood what my job was, and I have a feeling I was doing it wrong. After three months I stopped showing up. I didn't even bother quitting; I just didn't show up, and no one ever said anything.

My first real journalism job after that was at my local paper, *The East Hampton Star*. I was close with the family who owns that paper, so it wasn't some big victory that I got the job. At first it was just for the summer and I mostly covered Hamptons gala fund-raisers and stuff like that. Then I was like, "I think I kind of like this," and ended up staying. It was a weekly paper, and I had a beat covering the school board and local government. That was where I learned the basics of how to write a newspaper story.

After that I ended up going to Russia—another lucky break—for three years, where I worked at ABC News and then as a researcher at *The New York Times* in Moscow. I wrote several articles for the *Times* and also freelanced for *The Moscow Times* and for the *Central European Business Review*. As I prepared to return to the United States, I proclaimed to friends who were *New York Times* correspondents that I wanted to work at *The New York Times* back in the United States. They laughed. "You'll have to start at a small paper and work your way up," they explained. "That's how it goes." So I took their advice, and back in the United States I began sending out résumés and clips to small newspapers. I must admit I felt special: "Look at me! I've worked with the best! Of course I'm going to get a job at your small daily paper. Why wouldn't you hire me?"

But I applied to newspapers large and small, and no one wanted me. I remember sending an application to the *Daily News* because they had advertised a search for reporters fluent in a second language. They wanted to cover more "ethnic neighborhoods" in New York City. My pitch was like, "I can help you cover the Russian community in New York. There's a lot of money coming in with the changeover in the Russian government, and I speak Russian."

Two weeks later, I got a letter saying, "Thank you very much for your application. At this time, we're looking for reporters who speak a second language." Ugh.

Months went by. I felt so unmoored, like a failure. I met with the editor at *The Baltimore Sun,* who said he wouldn't hire me because I was too inexperienced but recommended I look into *The Times-Picayune* in New Orleans. The paper had recently won a Pulitzer and the editor was well-known.

I applied and was excited to be asked down for an interview! I was also scared because I had never been to the South and didn't know anything about Louisiana or New Orleans. I did my homework and tried to figure out the history of the paper and what it covered, reading as much as I could, while worrying about what I would wear. I remember going with my mom to buy an interview suit with a jacket and matching pants. *The Times-Picayune* flew me there and put me up in a hotel, which seemed fancy.

On the day of my interview, they drove me to one of the newspaper's bureaus, which was a strip-mall office in one of the parishes surrounding New Orleans. I remember not being totally clear what a parish was or how the local government worked, and pretending during my interview that I knew more than I did— not wanting to reveal how ignorant I was. Everything felt so rural and unfamiliar. It was a different culture from the one in which I'd been raised, but I thought, *This is a new thing to discover. I'll be like a foreign correspondent in the same way that I was in Russia!* And it was a small-town paper, but I would work my way up.

In the evening, people at the paper hooked me up to attend a party hosted at one of the reporters' apartments. I went and hung out with the people who would be my colleagues, and I liked them a lot. They were friendly and welcoming and seemed excited about what they were doing.

But soon after I flew back to New York, I learned that I hadn't gotten the job. And I was just gobsmacked. *They were so nice to me!* I thought.

Over the phone, I asked the *Times-Picayune* editors if they could give me any insight as to what had happened. They said something like "We want someone who's really dedicated to working in the bureau." Of course they wanted somebody who cared about the community and who wanted to stay. I thought, *No, no—I can be and* will *be that person.* But that was that.

Self-reflection is useful; self-recrimination is not. You have to keep going.

The interaction sent me into quite a spin. I suddenly wondered if I wasn't as qualified as I had thought, and whether I had come off as cocky or superior in some way. Had I been communicating that I thought I was too good to work there? Had I not been humble? "Who am I?" I wondered. "What kind of reporter am I going to be, and how can I communicate that?"

I've never been a cocky person; I'm too insecure to be genuinely cocky. But I think I had imagined, "Oh yeah, there's no way these people in Louisiana aren't going to want me." I had worked at *The New York Times*! I had this semi–stamp of approval (or thought I did) from the world's greatest newspaper (arguably).

The experience made me realize that whatever fairy dust falls on you because of *The New York Times,* it's like bullshit. You have to be good. It doesn't matter that *The New York Times* is good. It was like *The Times-Picayune* was saying, "Your airs are not only useless, but insulting." I didn't mean to have those airs, and honestly in retrospect, I don't know if I did. But my fear is that I was exuding some of that.

I was close with my elderly cousin, who was like a grandmother to me. We saw each other and wrote letters and talked on the phone. She lived in New York City, and I remember calling her and saying, "I didn't get it. I didn't get the *Times-Picayune* job." I was close to crying.

My cousin had been a teacher and a school principal in Harlem for many years and had this stentorian kind of bearing. In a commanding tone, she said, "You will *not* be blue." There was a pause. It was like she had slapped me across the face and said, "Stop being such a baby." And it actually helped. I needed to keep going, and I did. I continued with applications and eventually landed a job at a paper in New Hampshire.

I'm pretty honest with myself about my shortcomings. It's painful but it has been ultimately helpful to face them. However, dwelling on them and getting in a sort of depressive swirl of self-recrimination is not helpful. And I will say as I've gotten older, dealing with rejection has gotten much, much easier. Because I have found success in my chosen field, I'm much more secure.

For example, lately I have been auditioning occasionally for animated voice-over roles. My background is in theater, and I think it would be so much fun. But I've auditioned for these little things, and it's so humiliating. Not only have I not gotten accepted; I've not even gotten a "thanks for trying." Like, zero. But it's like, you know what? I don't give a shit. I'm going to try. Why not?

SARAH KOENIG'S TIPS

TIP 1—I think there's a balance between recognizing "What part did I play, and do I need to deal with that, as ugly as it might be?" and being like, "Just recognize it and keep going."

TIP 2—You know what would be bizarre? If you never failed and you never got rejected. And it probably wouldn't serve you well either, as a good human being.

JOAN WILLIAMS

I think men are better equipped to externalize a rejection because they're told consistently that they're friggin' awesome, whereas women, unless they've done a lot of cognitive-override work, are more likely to internalize it. When a woman receives a rejection, one of the things that happens is that she goes, "I knew I wasn't a fit for that job; I felt it in my bones." Because women hold these internalized biases too.

Joan Williams recalled giving an interview to a prominent reporter who was asking why she was interested in research about work-family conflict. "And I just said, 'Because I've lived through all of it.'" Williams has spent most of her career working to create new structures and policies to fight gender bias at work. She is a Distinguished Professor of Law, Hastings Foundation chair, and founding director of the Center for WorkLife Law at the University of California, Hastings College of the Law. Williams and her daughter, Rachel Dempsey, wrote the book *What Works for Women at Work*, which should be required reading for all humans.

In addition to her research on gender, Williams does a significant amount of work on social class. Her studies and writing have been deeply influential in academia, in the media, and in public policy. Williams's article in the *Harvard Business Review* "What So Many People Don't Get About the U.S. Working Class" was *HBR*'s most popular of all time, with more than 3 million reads.

Lessons I've Learned

It can be useful to listen to critiques like "You're not a team player" with an understanding that people at work may be more likely to say this kind of thing to women.

In my second year as a law professor, I was assigned to be on the law school admissions committee, which would mean reading hundreds of student applications. It would be incredibly time-consuming and burdensome, and furthermore, it was a low-status job at the institution. Working in admissions wouldn't help me to build my network, earn tenure, and gain job security. It was not a career-building opportunity.

I said no. How did I have the guts? Partly it was because I was clueless. I didn't understand the political implications of saying no, that's for sure. I just knew that the coin of the realm in academia was scholarship, and I wanted to be a scholar.

I later found out that another female law professor, Clare Dalton, had been assigned to be on the admissions committee when she was a junior professor at the same institution. Evidently they thought that very junior women were a perfect match for this work. (Clare Dalton ultimately sued for sex discrimination and won.)

Meanwhile, my saying no created a very unhealthy atmosphere for me at that school. I was seen as difficult and not a team player. I have since come to understand that this kind of powerful language is employed to whip women back where they belong. Our culture expects women to be communal: modest, self-effacing, nice, and interpersonally sensitive. Men are expected to be agentic: competitive, ambitious, direct, and assertive. We try to police women back into their proper roles by telling assertive women they're not good team players, but what that *really* means is that they're not good helpmates to the men. I was willing to deal with being seen as "not a team player" because I knew what it took to become a published and tenured law professor—it did not include reading admissions applications. But I also look back and think about how politically clueless I was when I was young; I had no idea that saying no would have repercussions.

When I started my career as a law professor, I studied local government law and environmental law. However, it gradually became clear that gender was totally determining the shape of my life both at work and at home. So I began to do "me-search," studying work-family issues and then the operation of gender bias in professional workplaces. I designed studies to examine how gender shapes the micropolitics of everyday life and (with my daughter and co-author, Rachel Dempsey) coined the term "the office housework" in *What Works for Women at Work*. Finally, the admissions work that I refused to do in my first job as a professor had a name.

My research also examined the ways in which women's behavior in biased workplaces was misinterpreted. For example, you may have heard media reports that "women don't negotiate," but the issue is actually more complex. Of course you should negotiate in some situations, but in others, you won't get what you want *and* you'll end up being disliked; it will be worse than if you had *never* negotiated. Another example of something you may have heard in the media: "Women allow themselves to be talked over by men." In fact, a woman may allow men to talk over her because she is politically savvy enough to know that doing otherwise would harm her status in the group. Unfortunately, one of the things that cements gendered behavior is women correctly assessing the level of gender bias in their environment. What is expected? What is frowned upon?

Studying gender hurt my career trajectory in very concrete ways. Even after I was a visiting professor at some very highly ranked institutions, I failed to get a job offer at another institution in my own city. (My husband's job kept us there.) After one search, a faculty member revealed that he had overheard members of his committee organizing against me because they did not like my work on gender. So I was stuck at the office-housework institution, being "difficult," for twenty-five years.

Don't get mad, get even.

The best advice I ever heard about getting over trouble and rejection was "Don't get mad, get even." I was outraged by the social construction of motherhood, so I helped found the field of work-family studies and created an area of law that allowed mothers (and, increasingly, fathers) to see if they were being discriminated against based on their caregiving responsibilities. I was outraged at the persistence of gender bias in professional workplaces, so I wrote *What Works for Women at Work* so that other women would not have to go through what I had gone through when I was so young and so unaided.

Don't accept a no-win situation.

At last I left the office-housework institution to join the faculty at my current institution, University of California, Hastings. For my entire professional life, I had been experiencing unhealthy gender dynamics, but at UC Hastings, the attitude was, "Let's celebrate the first female distinguished professor we've ever hired from the outside!"

"Oh, wait . . . you mean I'm not a bitch?"

I realized that women shouldn't have to put up with sexism at work. Women should be able to spot the kind of toxic environment that I had been living in for decades and say, "I'm outta here."

My husband and I agree that one of the big mistakes we made was not moving earlier. Once I was out of that bad work environment, I had space to think. I wasn't so embattled and angry. Not only did that improve my work life—it improved my home life too.

JOAN WILLIAMS'S TIPS

TIP 1—If a man is rejected and he goes back and says, "I'm not taking no for an answer," then he's seen as admirably persistent. Men are expected to be competitive and ambitious; there's more social room for a man to contest a rejection. If a woman contests a rejection, then *she just can't get the damn message:* "Who the hell does she think she is?" It won't work, and she'll be seen as someone who's difficult. Here is my advice: If you're doing something that violates prescriptive stereotypes—doing something typically seen as "masculine"—then do it in a feminine way by upping the level of warmth in your tone and expression.

TIP 2—If you are feeling awful at work, don't discount the possibility that you could be experiencing the effects of sexism or racism or both. Our work contexts (and the people in them) really impact how we feel day to day at our jobs.

LAURA WEIDMAN POWERS

> You never know the degree to which sexism and racism are actually impacting you in any given moment, but we can be certain they impact us over the course of our careers and within our communities.

Still in her thirties, Laura Weidman Powers has earned a long list of awards and accolades: She's been included on the *Ebony* Power 100 List; *Foreign Policy* magazine gave her a Global Thinker award; the Root *twice* named her one of the Root 100, the list of most influential African Americans.

Laura graduated from Harvard and earned a joint MBA and JD from Stanford, but when I contacted her about this project, she'd left her executive-level job and was traveling around the world with her husband and one-year-old daughter. She e-mailed back, "Happy to do an interview. I'll be in Valencia, Spain, from April 15 to May 15 so that would be a good stretch to schedule something."

In an article on Medium, Laura wrote about the "nerd girls" weekend that had catalyzed the family trip. In the fall of 2017, she and female peers from Stanford business school gathered for their third annual weekend of reflection, connection, and conversation, which included coming up with at least one "wild" life dream. Laura's dream was becoming a travel writer—and the group thought this was doable, at least in a way. "Having eight smart, in-tune, empathetic, analytical, supportive women coaching you through the path to your wildest dreams is a pretty incredible experience," Laura wrote. "When I got in my car at the end of the weekend to drive up to San Francisco, I knew with certainty that my husband and I would both quit our jobs and we would travel for an extended period of time. And I would blog about it."

Now she has returned home and is living in Brooklyn, working as the head of impact at Echoing Green, which invests in and supports emerging social entrepreneurs around the world—Laura herself was an Echoing Green fellow in 2013.

She has worked in and helped to start companies in both the for-profit and not-for-profit sectors. She was co-founder of Code2040, a nonprofit aimed at changing the racial composition of tech companies by the year 2040. As CEO, Laura grew the company from an idea to a seven-million-dollar organization with thirty-five staff members.

In 2016, the Obama administration invited her to be a senior advisor to Chief Technology Officer Megan Smith. In her six-month term at the White House, Laura focused on issues of diversity and inclusion in the tech industry.

Lessons I've Learned

A rejection in the moment feels so dramatic because it's what is right in front of you. But I don't even think about my rejection from Google anymore.

In 2011, I was newly married and newly unemployed, which was a terrible combination for my mental health. My husband had a job at a law firm and would work ninety-hour weeks, coming home so fried that all he could do was sit and watch football on Sunday afternoons. I hate football. I was going nuts. I'd always worked and had been an executive at a tech company in Los Angeles but moved to San Francisco to be with him when my company started to flounder. Now, instead of enjoying the opportunity to leisurely consider what I wanted to do next in my career, I was spending all day looking at jobs, sending off résumés to whatever seemed remotely like a fit, and having coffee with people in order to network.

One coffee meeting was with a business school classmate named Tristan Walker. He wanted to start an organization aimed at breaking down systemic barriers for black and Latinx people in tech and wanted me to take the CEO role. He thought we'd work well together. I believed in his mission but wasn't sure I wanted to go down this road. I'd built start-ups before, but now I had law and business degrees, and ideally I wanted a good job with benefits. I told him I'd think about it.

Meanwhile, I sent an application to Google for a role as the internal communications person for David Drummond.

Drummond was a Google executive who'd been involved since the beginning. I wasn't totally clear on what the job was or whether I'd find it interesting, but there was such prestige and appeal in landing at Google. It had great brand recognition and a reputation for being a collection of very smart people. It was employee-friendly, with lots of perks and benefits. I also liked the notion of being able to work with someone who was really senior, learning about the company from that vantage point.

The first couple of interviews at Google went well. I felt like my answers to their questions were good, and they seemed to like me. I was hopeful that this would work out, and when I thought about working there versus on the start-up with Tristan, I thought, *How could I turn down Google's benefits, pay, and prestige?*

But I was nervous going into my third interview. I still wasn't clear on what the actual job was. The person interviewing me was a white woman in her thirties, very confident and only mildly interested in me. I'd brought a change of shoes to put on just before going in but realized three minutes into talking with her that I had forgotten to change and was wearing the wrong ones. I felt like my outfit was off, the conversation was off. We just weren't vibing.

I didn't feel great when I left the interview, and I didn't get an offer. It was super-discouraging. By this time, I had sent out a zillion résumés and had gotten very few responses. What was I not bringing to the table?

I sensed that potential employers thought I was overqualified for some jobs; for some others, they didn't see my qualifications as a fit. But I had a degree from Harvard and two degrees from

Stanford, with work experience in and outside of the tech sector, and it still was not the right profile. It was like there was some puzzle or riddle that I was supposed to unlock or solve, but I couldn't figure out what it was. I felt so depressed and rejected but also convinced that if they just said yes and gave me a shot, I would be awesome at it.

The more I hit wall after wall, the more I was like, "Well, one person—Tristan—seems to think I'm pretty talented. Maybe I should go work with *that* person as opposed to trying to talk these other people into hiring me." The idea of just jumping in and having something to do became more and more appealing, and I was confident that I could do a good job of getting the organization off the ground.

My initial thinking was that I would team up with Tristan, set up the operations and programs for eighteen months, and hand it off to someone else to run. But we launched Code2040 and got so much traction during the first year that it was clear we'd tapped into a moment. The organization was new, its model untested, but prominent people wanted to join our board. Companies and universities wanted to partner with us. Every conversation ended with "Tell me how I can get involved." It turned out that everyone had been having conversations in their heads about why the tech industry was so white and male and homogenous; nobody was having that conversation out loud. Then we showed up and said something out loud and people were like, "Finally!" The vision and mission of the organization quickly grew, and it became exciting.

The narrative at the time was that tech was a meritocracy and that it wasn't diverse was because of pipelines: *There just isn't a diverse enough pool of qualified black, Latinx, indigenous, or female candidates!* We set out to prove that wrong through our fellows program, a career accelerator for computer science students from underrepresented groups. We supported them in getting internships, ensured their success, and helped them to get full-time offers. That piece of our work was extremely successful. We were changing the lives of hundreds of students and connecting them to opportunity and wealth building and all this great stuff, but it became clear that the real problem was much bigger.

Certain hiring practices were keeping diverse talent out; for example, companies would get so many résumés that they'd end up sorting via seemingly simple categories, like "top ten colleges and universities." That left out historically black colleges and universities and Hispanic-serving institutions. Another example: Job descriptions called for "rock stars" and "ninjas," using the language of combat or celebrity. These presumed a level of individualism and confidence that often felt off-putting to folks from underrepresented backgrounds. Even office common spaces—which played certain music and offered particular games—gave the message that these were companies designed for twenty-four-year-old white male engineers. There was no *one* element where you'd say, "This is race- or sex-based," but collectively the systems, policies, and practices heavily prioritized white male culture. We realized that if we wanted to meaningfully shift the composition of these companies, we'd have to retool the way they operated, and that work was the next step in our development of Code2040.

Looking back on my own short stretch of unemployment, I think I was in some ways ignorant about the biases that were baked into the hiring processes and into popular notions of what talent looked like. It's obvious from my résumé that I'm a woman. It probably was obvious that I'm black because I had things like the Harvard Black Students Association on there. Of course, there's all sorts of research about how that decreases your likelihood of getting an interview. But I still was in a headspace of just taking it really personally and not situating it in a broader pattern.

Years after starting and running Code2040, I got to know David Drummond—the guy I'd been applying to work for at Google. One time, I said something to his assistant (whom I also got to know) about how I had interviewed to be the internal communications person for David Drummond. She was like, "We've never had that role on our team." I don't know if they just ended up not hiring for it; by the time I brought it up, it was six years after the fact. But I did think it was so ironic that I ended up building that connection and relationship in a totally different way.

LAURA WEIDMAN POWERS'S TIPS

TIP 1—I think the Google job just felt like such a big deal at the time because it was the major thing that was staring me in the face. But it's important to remember that we don't live in a world where all opportunities are presented at the exact same time for you to choose from. A rejection happens, and then other opportunities come later.

TIP 2—If things feel off at work, if you sense that bias is affecting your experience, then make sure you plug yourself into communities and opportunities that value you and your worth, even as you may try to change the system.

LAURA HUANG

When Harvard called me and asked if I was interested
in moving and joining them on their faculty, I was sort
of shocked. And I even sort of said something along
the lines of "You *do* realize you've rejected me three
times already?"

Laura Huang, a Harvard Business School professor, told me
that she had been rejected so many times that it would be
hard to decide on a story to tell for this book. "I have hundreds of
rejection stories," she said. "I have the story of when I was younger
and I was rejected from the gifted-and-talented program. I have
the story of being rejected from multiple schools. I have rejections
from jobs. I have a rejection from last week!"

But she also told me that she had been very shy growing up. I
wondered: As a shy person, how did she put herself out there, taking all these risks that (sometimes) led to rejection? Huang said,
"Over time, I found ways to take action that fit with my personality.
For example, instead of asserting myself and saying, 'I think this!'
I would ask a question like 'Why do people think this?' I developed
a repertoire of ways to take action that fit who I was and who I am."

Laura Huang's first book is *Edge: Turning Adversity into Advantage,* which was published in 2020. Before teaching at Harvard, she was a professor at the Wharton School of Business at the
University of Pennsylvania. Her research is on interpersonal

relationships and implicit bias in entrepreneurship and in the workplace, and it has been written about all over, including in *The Wall Street Journal, USA Today, Forbes,* and *Nature.*

Lessons I've Learned

Tracking rejections can help you find informative patterns.

The development of my career has not been linear. It's had stops and starts, zigs and zags. I didn't know what I wanted to be when I grew up, and I still don't—I don't know that I will be a Harvard professor for the rest of my life.

As the child of immigrants, I spent time going back and forth between Taiwan and the United States. I was not good at many things when I was young: I wasn't athletic or musical. I was painfully shy and didn't have many friends. At Duke University, I majored in engineering, but that didn't come naturally either—it always felt like I was forcing it. Maybe it was because I was always working so much: I had my work-study placements plus a twenty-hour-a-week job on the side. But I finally graduated with an engineering degree and went to build servers for IBM. After that, I worked at Johnson & Johnson, and a manager encouraged me to apply to business school.

It was at business school that I started doing research with a professor and realized that I loved it. I had never known that a career in academia was even possible, and now I wanted to keep doing research—but of course, I had tons of student loans to pay off.

I kept asking everyone, "What's the quickest way to pay off student loans?" They'd say, "Go into I-banking," but I had no idea what "I-banking" was. I remember turning to a friend and being like, "Wow, this internet banking thing is a big deal!" Of course, it turned out that "I-banking" meant investment banking. I worked in investment banking for two years to pay off the loans, and on my two-year anniversary, I quit to start a PhD program at the University of California, Irvine, studying organizational behavior and entrepreneurship.

My first faculty placement was at the Wharton School at the University of Pennsylvania. The only way to progress in academia is by getting published, but the publication rate is abysmally low, especially in top-tier publications. At first, I felt nearly paralyzed by that fact.

One day, a senior and very accomplished professor in my department—someone who had published tons of articles— asked me, "How are things going?"

I told him, "I just want *one* paper accepted at a top-tier publication, so I can prove to myself and everyone else that it wasn't a fluke I got this job."

He said to me, "Well, I had eighteen rejections before I had a single acceptance."

I was shocked *and* encouraged. I made a rule for myself to try for eighteen rejections. Every time I got one, I would write the name of the article that was rejected on a piece of paper that I hung on my wall. Interestingly, I started noticing patterns: A particular paper would *keep* getting rejected, or one that I wrote with certain co-authors—even those who were fairly senior, who I thought knew what they were doing—would be repeatedly rejected, and I was actually doing better co-authoring with colleagues at my same career stage.

Trying for those eighteen rejections gave me permission to take risks, to even seek out rejection. The experimentation allowed me to learn. There was data, and things that I could learn, in each of those rejections.

Even embarrassment can serve as data: I learned to network in a way that felt comfortable.

When I first joined the faculty at Wharton, a colleague told me, "It's really important that you network. Meet the senior associate deans, associate deans, and senior faculty."

I was like, "What? How do I do that?"

He said, "Well, go to drinks or grab dinner. You don't have to have an agenda, you just want to get to know them."

So I started asking senior associate deans and senior faculty, "Do you want to grab lunch?" I would try to get on their schedule and sometimes it would take a while.

There was this one senior associate dean with whom it took weeks to schedule a meeting. Finally, we sat down together over lunch. He looked at me and asked, "So, what do you want to talk about? What's your agenda?"

I was like, "Oh, I don't have an agenda; I just wanted to get to know you."

I remember the expression on his face. It was like, *What?! I'm a really important man. If you invited me to lunch, it's because you had an agenda—talking about the state of the university or the teaching curriculum or the annual fund. Something really important.*

And that lunch went disastrously. The conversation was stilted and I felt completely self-conscious. There were huge gaps of silence as we each chewed our food. I felt rejected and embarrassed.

I avoided him for the next three weeks. But then I was flying to a conference to give a talk and he ended up being on the same plane. As we were getting off, he saw me and asked, "Oh, hey. Are you going to this conference?" I said that I was, and he asked, "How are you getting there?"

"I'll probably just take a taxi," I said, because the conference was at this hotel forty-five minutes away.

"I have a private car waiting," he said. "Do you want to join me?" At first I said no, thank you, but he offered again and I accepted the ride. We traveled together to the conference for forty-five minutes, and this time, there didn't need to be an agenda. We talked about our families, our values, and it was a lot more comfortable than the lunch had been. We developed a rapport, and to this day, he's one of the people I'll call if I want help problem solving or if I need a mentor. It's because it wasn't forced; I wasn't "networking" with him in a way that I'd tried to before.

Part of rejection is embarrassment; in fact, there can be a lot of data in embarrassment. Why does this rejection sting for you when it might not for someone else? (Or why are you *not* embarrassed when another person would be?) Embarrassment teaches you about your own values, what you believe in and care about. That's important, because it allows you to propel yourself forward in a different way.

What I learned from the embarrassment of that disastrous lunch is that asking out unknown colleagues is not my thing. It doesn't feel authentic to me. What makes sense for me is getting to know people in a more organic way, so if there's someone that I want to get to know, I might join a committee that person is on, for example, and then show how I provide value—offering opinions, asking questions, being myself as part of the beginning of a potential relationship with that person.

Years later, I published my first book, *Edge: Turning Adversity into Advantage.* I believe that some people naturally have an advantage, but other people have to create one for themselves. It really is possible to do that in an authentic way.

LAURA HUANG'S TIPS

TIP 1—I went into investment banking, and on my two-year anniversary of starting at the bank, I quit and started a PhD program. My student loans were paid off. One of the things I tell a lot of my students is that we all have responsibilities and sometimes there are things we have to do. That doesn't mean we can't do what we *want to do* later. It's okay to wait.

TIP 2—I look for "data" in my rejections, categorizing them based on emotions I felt (embarrassment versus anger versus sadness) instead of the normal categories that we think of (work rejections versus personal rejections, etc.). When I look for patterns across different emotions, I find that I learn a lot more about myself.

MARILYN CARLSON NELSON

Understand that when you ask people to make a change, at first there's rejection and then sometimes there's anger.

When Marilyn Carlson Nelson graduated from Smith College in 1961 with a degree in economics, it was hard to find jobs beyond secretary, teacher, or nurse. After some searching, she landed a job as a junior stock analyst at Paine Webber, but the company told her to sign her name as "M. C. Nelson." They said that no one would buy stock from a woman.

Eventually, she married, had children, and left Paine Webber to work in her family's marketing company. Her supervisor—not a family member—was so impressed by her skills that he asked her to lead a division. When she excitedly went to her father to tell him about her promotion, his response shocked her. Carlson Nelson's father said that such a big job was "inappropriate" for a mother of small children.

"I remember having tears in my eyes," she told me, "and going down the office's back stairs. I went from being elated about my promotion to being devastated and literally fired."

She went home and ultimately had two more children. But once they were in school, she began taking volunteer jobs. She would prove to her father that she not only belonged in the family business but could lead it. Over the next decade, her volunteer responsibilities grew until she was heading up projects with multimillion-dollar budgets. City leaders in Minneapolis urged her to run for governor or US Senate. Carlson Nelson's father relented, finally understanding the scope of her ambition. "If you're willing to make those kinds of sacrifices," he said, "then I think you should come into the company."

It took her many years to get over her father's rejection, she told me, but once she was back in the family global travel, hotel, restaurant, and marketing business, she didn't disappoint, ultimately becoming the company's CEO. She held that role for ten years.

Lessons I've Learned

When you are trying to make change as a leader,
you will get pushback.

In the early 2000s, I went to Sweden for a global meeting on fighting child sex trafficking. The Carlson Family Foundation had co-founded the World Childhood Foundation and I had been asked to talk about our efforts to help the homeless youth population known as "street children." Our foundation worked to get these kids in school, teach them skills, and find them shelter. But at that meeting, I learned something new about homeless children: They were extremely vulnerable to being trafficked. I heard horrifying stories about a growing problem and about how the internet was enabling it. There were actual tours to Thailand

and Cambodia—mostly for men, who were "promised" a certain number of children.

Not long after the conference, I had a call from the US ambassador to Bangladesh, Earl R. Miller, who asked me to come to Washington to talk specifically about trafficking. Because my company, Carlson, had hotels all over the world, Miller thought we could be leaders in making an impact. Trafficked children were often taken across borders and into various hotels and motels. He explained that not a single North American travel or hospitality company had joined up with End Child Prostitution and Trafficking (ECPAT) and he asked if we would be the first. While I wanted to say yes right away, I was concerned that taking the lead on this issue would give the impression that trafficking was a particular problem at our hotels. I told Ambassador Miller that I would need to inspire the support of my executive team.

In a way, I felt called to make this commitment, as I remembered a day soon after my first grandson had been born. My daughter had come with the baby to visit Minnesota from New York, where they lived. One night, the baby was sleeping, and I encouraged my daughter to get some rest, saying I would tend to him when he woke. He slept for longer than I had expected. Finally, I heard him. The cradle was by a window facing east, and I lifted him out just around dawn. The sun was rising, shining behind his head, and it almost looked like he had a halo. I had this rush of love and felt like he was just fresh from God, with his little head up against my neck.

In some ways I have thought of this moment as an epiphany, because as I held him, I realized that I couldn't protect him. It didn't matter if I was a CEO of a big global company. I couldn't build walls tall enough or locks strong enough to keep him from meeting people who had *not* had anyone to lift them lovingly out of their cradles, people who had had traumatic childhoods and were full of anger. I realized that the best thing I could do for my grandson would be to care about those other children as well.

Recalling that insight gave me extra courage to go back to our company and tell the executive team that we needed to join with ECPAT. It meant that we would go public with our commitment, training people at all our hotels on what to watch for and how to call and report potential trafficking. We would work with our supply chain and make it clear that we didn't do business with people or companies who trafficked, either in sex or in labor. And we would make it clear to not only our employees but our customers as well that we were helping to raise awareness about this problem.

The executive team's first reaction was extremely negative. The public relations person told me, "No way." The company lawyers said, "We have a thousand hotels across the world; what if somewhere, a concierge facilitates a child trafficking incident and we're held accountable? We'll be publicly embarrassed! You're making us more vulnerable!"

I told the public relations people and the lawyers that they should go home and think about it, saying, "Not knowing about this problem was kind of a blessing. We didn't feel compelled to play a role in solving it. But now we know, and we are leaders in our industry."

In a few days, the PR person came back to me. He had talked to some employees and said he was surprised—the employees were proud that I was thinking about this. It made them feel good about working for us. Instead of being shocked, they thought that a commitment to prevent child trafficking would underscore the sense that we were a caring global company. They were excited to engage, to help.

And then the lawyer came back. He said, "Our company already signs on to comply with US anti-corruption practices, and this is a corrupt practice. You have my support."

When advocating for change, identify multiple routes that will get you where you want to go.

We joined ECPAT and began training our people in different ways, depending on their jobs. For example, at the hotel front desk, employees note if someone shows up with a child who doesn't meet their eyes. Housekeeping staff watch for young girls who are very heavily made up and sexily dressed. Ultimately, we, the Carlson Family Foundation, funded Polaris, a hotline for trafficking victims or people who witness trafficking. A victim who calls can get picked up from any location very quickly. If a hotel calls, Polaris connects them with the police department or with another response organization.

We began working with other groups beyond our hotels, for example, Airline Ambassadors, an association of flight attendants who talked about feeling helpless when they observed suspicious-looking situations—a child coming on the plane with no toys or with an adult who seemed unrelated to the child. They joined the fight. Ultimately, Delta Air Lines joined ECPAT.

But I knew we needed to do more. As president (at that time) of the Travel Industry of America, I spoke about child trafficking at the major travel industry meeting. While the Travel Industry of America voted to oppose human trafficking, no other individual company was ready to join ECPAT. It was almost nine years before anyone else in the industry actually joined.

Even when people didn't join, we were still able to make them partners. Early on, I went to Bill Marriott, because I consider him a deeply caring person; Marriott is a family business. He told me, "We don't sign things," and he clearly had the same concerns that our PR people and lawyers had originally expressed. I urged him to at least engage in the discussion. That's what was important. He did and ended up training his employees. I wasn't surprised a couple of years later when I heard him make a conference presentation where he urged others to step up. I felt grateful because he's a real leader in the industry and I knew he would move things forward.

Our legal counsel, the man who had been so cautious at first, ended up connecting me with the American Bar Association, which today has representatives designated to help companies put anti-trafficking language into corporate codes of conduct. Engaging with child sex trafficking is a corrupt practice, and companies began to see that. We were gradually turning the conversation around so that the reputational risk was for those who *didn't* take a stand, rather than those who did.

People resist when you're trying to do something that makes them uncomfortable. Then slowly, with good data, people start to adapt. It's important to be aware that as a change agent, you are the catalyst for a process that can take time. It's vital to keep from becoming so frustrated that you lose the opportunity to make a difference. It's vital to have patience and the facts.

MARILYN CARLSON NELSON'S TIPS

TIP 1—When you are trying to make a change, acknowledge that whatever the pushback, there is often validity in other people's concerns. Show respect for different opinions. But repeat the facts as you know them.

TIP 2—It helps to listen and find ways to reposition your argument, showing that it also meets the other person's objectives. That way, they don't have to be on the defensive.

PART 2

Creativity Is on the Other Side

My friend Arielle Eckstut knew she wanted to run her own business from the time she was seven and her second grade operated a real fruit and vegetable market, buying wholesale from suppliers downtown and setting up shop to sell apples and zucchinis in the school hallway. Arielle has always been industrious, creative, and stylish, so I wasn't surprised by her brilliant first business endeavor, LittleMissMatched.

LittleMissMatched is a company all about inspiring creativity and individuality in tween girls, who, as Arielle phrases it, exist "between little-kid freedom and the oppression of teenage-hood, where you have to follow what everyone else does." The company sells beautiful, hip socks—black backgrounds, rainbow polka dots or stripes—in groups of three, inviting kids to make their own combinations. Arielle was the creative vision, the person behind the design and color and inventive ideas, such as whiteboard-like furniture that invited kids to draw on it. Her business partner was a man whose expertise was sales.

LittleMissMatched was so successful that a major private equity firm invested at around the same time that Arielle went on maternity leave with her newborn daughter (a leave her male business partner referred to as her "vacation"). While she was on leave, the equity firm installed that male partner as CEO, telling Arielle that she would henceforth be director of marketing.

"It made no sense whatsoever," Arielle says, looking back, "but I'm someone who naturally thinks, *Titles don't matter, let's just do good work*." It was a demotion, though, and was disheartening. Eventually, she was pushed out of the company altogether.

"There was definitely a very negative downward spiral after that rejection," Arielle recalls, "but it was also liberating because I had gradually become miserable there." Still, it wasn't like creativity emerged right away; Arielle remembers that it took a while to reenergize the creative side of herself. (One thing that helped her to recover was that the company flailed without her. "Sometimes you don't get that kind of reinforcement," she said, "but I did.")

It also helped to forge creative partnerships. Arielle says, "If I have someone else cheerleading or inspiring me, getting the juices flowing, my creativity kicks into gear and rejection fades to the background." In collaboration with her mom, Joann, she wrote a gorgeous book called *The Secret Language of Color* and a follow-up titled *What Is Color?* With her husband, David, she started a business called The Book Doctors, which nurtures authors through writing and publishing. Arielle and David started speaking and traveling, bringing their daughter, Olive—who at age twelve has now been to thirty-seven states. On one trip, Arielle met the children's book writer Kwame Alexander; they're also business partners now, developing children's books and television shows.

Arielle's LittleMissMatched rejection ultimately led to other creative projects; in fact, rejection can *make* some people more creative. This is borne out in research, and I saw it in multiple interviewees. Singer Rachel Platten was almost *fueled* by rejection; it led to her producing her own album and to the breakout hit "Fight Song," which climbed music charts around the world. Actress Alysia Reiner produced her own movie. CEO Polly Rodriguez got tired of working at a sexist start-up and decided to launch her own company.

After a rejection, it can take time to find the uniquely helpful thing that unlocks your creativity. Arielle says that for her, partnering was the key to being creative, but "everyone has a different key."

RACHEL PLATTEN

Beautiful art comes from when you let your inner artist be wild and unafraid rather than judging her.

Rachel Platten told me that when she was growing up, she
wasn't a standout vocalist. No one ever said, "Hey, you should
think about following music as a career." She took piano lessons
and sang with her family but also loved math. She attended Trin-
ity College in Connecticut, where she was an international relations major.

Then her path changed, and Platten worked very, very hard
on the new direction. I had always imagined Top 40 singers to
be "selected"—through luck, connections, or magic—by record
companies. I imagined that the companies offered songs to these
magically chosen singers, and then the singers recorded them,
and voilà! Smash hit. But I was wrong. Platten worked with commitment and passion for more than a decade before success came,
writing thousands of songs. If you watch the video for her hit
"Fight Song," you'll see it's really about the perseverance she had,
persisting in the face of rejection, playing one show after another.
(Also, if you are a parent, watch Rachel's video for the song "You
Belong," which shares a title with her recently published first
children's book. Have tissues nearby.)

Rachel Platten's "Fight Song" became an international sensation; she won an Emmy for performing it on the *Today* show. Her records have gone multiplatinum. But she is lovely and down-to-earth and was very open to talking about the rejections along her path.

Lessons I've Learned

Major, heartbreaking disappointments can happen on the path to success.

During my junior year abroad, I traveled to Trinidad to attend the University of the West Indies and learn about Carnival. Internships were part of the experience, and I got to intern at a record label. One day, a recording artist called the label to say he was looking for a substitute backup singer who could play keyboards. He had a big show that night and his keyboardist was sick. I had grown up playing piano and had always sung informally with my family; I surprised myself by volunteering.

That night changed my life. Onstage, looking out at the crowd, I felt a sense of joy and purpose. I wanted it to be *my* crowd. There was this electric aha moment: "This is it. This is what I'm supposed to be doing with my life."

I started learning guitar and writing songs immediately and, after graduation, moved to New York City, where I freelanced, waitressed, and filled notebooks with lists of small goals: *play the Canal Room; have 10 songs.* There were small rejections all the time: I would try booking a show and wouldn't get it; I'd send a demo to a manager but would never hear back. It might hurt for a moment, but I'd keep going, like, "Okay, what can I do today? Practice piano. Meet up with a friend and write a song. Go to a club and check out another artist to see if that's a vibe for me." I kept myself really busy.

When I was about twenty-five, I met my husband. He changed my life, both because I fell in love and because he believed in me and thought I should work harder. I started practicing piano at all hours of the night; I honed my guitar skills. I'd been writing a song a month, but I increased that to ten songs a month and found that you can exercise creativity like a muscle. I showed up every day, whether the muse did or not. Some days nothing would happen, but other days I was ready with my voice warmed up, my fingers on the piano, and wrote something I liked.

I built a community of artists in New York, and we'd all come together and play on Tuesday nights at a bar on MacDougal Street. These were some incredible people, with whom I'm still close. They taught me that when I was onstage, I should pay close attention to what was happening internally. It wasn't about what other people thought.

I also started volunteering with a program called Musicians on Call, where musicians play bedside for hospital patients. That was transformative because I was able to let go of my ego and be reminded of what my music could do. Sometimes I was on critical care wards where patients had severe brain trauma, and a nurse would tell me, "Oh, this patient blinked" or "He's moving his hand." I'd leave the hospital feeling like I'd been thrown a lifeline, a way to stay mindful about what was important to me, which was connection and healing through music.

Every Monday, Wednesday, and Friday night, I'd play three

hours of covers with a couple of originals sprinkled in, and I started to build a little following. One of my fans was a publicist who encouraged me to put out an album myself. I followed her advice; she loved the songs and asked if she could send it to a small indie label she knew.

They signed me, sent me on a low-key tour, and also played my song "A Thousand Ships" for a radio promo guy. He liked it so much that they decided to do a radio campaign for the song. You tour around the country visiting radio stations, bringing pizza, shaking hands, and saying, "This is my song. I'm Rachel. Will you play it?" And you perform your song in a conference room. I'd spent seven years playing bars, trying to get sports-watching patrons to pay attention, so I knew how to work a crowd, and the radio stations started playing my music.

The songs climbed the charts, bigger labels took notice, and RCA called. They wanted to sign me! This had been my ultimate goal, and I was so excited. I met the whole team and they proposed a deal. I would finally have a little money; I'd have a tour bus.

Then right before I signed the contract, I had a show and could sense that my manager was acting weird before I went onstage. He asked if we could talk afterward. We went back to my Manhattan apartment and I remember sitting on my living room couch in our tiny fifth-floor walkup on MacDougal Street, ready to talk about the RCA deal. But it turned out that RCA had been watching the charts, seeing my songs falling, and had gotten cold feet. They'd taken the deal off the table. My manager had been waiting to give me the bad news. I remember feeling so shocked, like the wind had been knocked out of me. My dream was dashed. I was back to the beginning.

Doubling down on yourself and working harder than you ever thought possible can help you get through rejection.

That was a turning point. I was in my early thirties and all my friends were starting to have babies, getting houses, getting on with their lives. I decided that I needed to really commit, to spend time in Los Angeles and Nashville, because that's where professional songwriting was happening. I had a music publishing deal; it wouldn't get my songs on the radio, but it could get the music and lyrics used in an advertisement or by another artist. My publisher introduced me to professional songwriters and I doubled down, living in LA for four years while my husband stayed in New York, working harder than ever on my writing.

"Fight Song" came to me after a phone conversation with my publisher. He'd said to me, "Just tell your story," and my story was that I was a fighter; I'd persisted in the face of so much rejection and disappointment. When I sent him the chorus, he said, "This is it. This is your fire. This is your song."

The following is kind of a streamlined version of what happened next, because for various reasons, it was actually a struggle to finish the song and get it produced. I finally recorded it myself and put it online. When I learned that my publisher had gotten me a placement for it on the popular TV show *Pretty Little Liars,* I knew *that* would be my moment. "Fight Song" was played on the episode, and I sat there waiting for—something. Action on Twitter, e-mails, some kind of explosion to happen.

Nothing happened. I remember that night was the closest I've ever been to giving up. I just started uncontrollably sobbing and just being like, "It's been thirteen years. I have poured everything into this."

I woke up the next morning and I was like, "Well, that was a lot of ego, Rachel. What the hell? What do you expect to happen? Get over it." Volunteering in hospitals, I already saw that people connected to my music, that it helped them, so why did I need it to happen on a massive level? *Relax,* I told myself. *Get another job and play music on the side. It's going to be beautiful.*

But a week later, a woman who had breast cancer randomly heard the song. Her brother was a radio DJ in Baltimore, and she said to him, "You have to put this on the radio. This is the most healing thing I've ever heard."

To honor her, he put it on the radio that weekend, and it shot to number one in Baltimore and the surrounding areas. Suddenly, every single label that had rejected me over and over started calling.

At the time, I was on tour, driving through the snow in my van to play a house concert in Ohio. My manager called. "Where are you?" he said. "Get to LA."

I was like, "I'm in Ohio. I have an important concert."

He said, "No, no, no. You don't understand what's going on." Within twenty-four hours, I was in LA at Snoop Dogg's Grammy party. I was signed to Columbia Records twenty-four hours after that. My song was on the radio two weeks after that. I sang at the Radio Disney Music Awards and then onstage with Taylor Swift. My song went to number one all around the country and in a couple of other countries too. It was a wild, wild journey.

I'm working on an album right now and I'm writing a song every day, getting back to the practice of nurturing my inner artist. There's so much obsession when you have a dream. You think, *I need this particular kind of success in order to be happy.* I'm catching myself in the loop again, but now I'm wiser and I see how it creeps in. I use meditation to ground myself and also to remember, yeah, it's not about what you need in order to be happy. It's what you already have.

RACHEL PLATTEN'S TIPS

TIP 1—After a rejection, you have to stop your own destructive narration, the looping story in which you tell yourself what just happened. The way to do that is through creativity itself. That's what breaks up the noise in your head and gets you back to your heart.

TIP 2—Volunteering is one of the best possible ways to overcome a failure, because all of a sudden you're not focused on what you don't have. You're focused on all that you can give.

TIP 3—Treat your inner artist like a kindergartener in art class. Be gentle rather than critical. Go back to the basics and remember the simple joy of singing around a campfire if you're a musician, or playing piano for a group of friends.

ELIZABETH BELL

I don't remember telling my parents that I got into medical school, and I guess that's significant, because I don't think they were jumping up and down with happiness.

Elizabeth Bell* loves her job as a psychiatrist in a big city. "When you're clicking along and simpatico with a patient, and he or she is able to make use of the work you're doing together, there's nothing like it," she told me. "It's so thrilling to be able to help somebody alter her course that way." It's fascinating, she says, to hear the stories her patients tell about themselves and then to put the stories together in a way that makes sense to the patients. They can then decide what they want to do. She tells her patients that she is not in the advice business but in the "get to know how your mind works" business. Patients can make use of what they learn about themselves and employ it or not, but it will be a conscious choice.

Bell sees patients approximately fifty hours a week. She also supervises psychiatry residents and students at a psychoanalytic institute, and she has had a number of roles at the medical school she attended. On the medical student promotions committee, she helps

* I have changed her name to maintain her privacy.

to evaluate students in trouble (either academically or as a result of some major violation). "I really enjoy that," she told me, "because there are not a lot of psychiatrists on the committee, and it's useful to help them understand how mental illness can impact behavior. Like, why would you fail a course for reasons other than that you're stupid? I knew from personal experience that it was possible."

Lessons I've Learned

There's more than one way to reach a goal.

I graduated from college in the late 1960s and got a job as a high school English teacher. I was always telling my twelfth graders, "Do what you really want to do," but at some point, I realized that *I* wasn't doing what I wanted. My husband and I were friends with a doctor couple. The wife was an intern in pediatrics and I was so jealous of her. I imagined myself writing prescriptions. I could wear a white coat. I'd have "MD" after my name. What it really boiled down to was that I could *be* something—I could have a kind of stature but also do something valuable.

Then my first child was born, and I left teaching. I was trying to decide what to do next, and one day I was driving to take a pottery course. My infant daughter was in the car and I thought, *I want to go to medical school. If I could become a doctor, I could take my profession anywhere. No matter what happens to me, I would have a way to make a living doing interesting work.*

I decided I would just take some premed requirements at a local college and see what happened. I had never been a great student, but the local public college was inexpensive and I figured if I failed, it wouldn't be a big financial loss. I registered for classes and hired a college student babysitter to come two afternoons a week so I could study at the library.

In General Chemistry, there was a group of students like me, older than the undergraduates, taking this course at night. We were all women; I was the only one with a child. They would come to my house and sit around the dining room table. My daughter would be at the table too, in her stroller, and we would eat dinner and go over the material. There was real camaraderie. We contributed to one another's knowledge, and I discovered—it may seem obvious—that studying actually made a difference. I got an A, then took the rest of the premed requirements: calculus, organic chemistry, and physics. (I'd taken biology in college.) Calculus sort of floated in and out of my mind—I could never fully get a grip on it—and the teacher said, "If you think you're going to just memorize formulas and pass this course, forget it. You will fail." But I did memorize the formulas; it was the best I could do. And I actually got an A.

Then our whole group applied to medical school. I applied to seventeen schools up and down the Eastern Seaboard; my husband was supportive and willing to move. My parents were not exactly supportive. My father had grown up an orphan and had always wanted to be a doctor, but in the early twentieth century, it was very hard for Jews to get into medical school. I think he had a lot of mixed feelings about my actually doing it. But I applied and then I waited, drunk on the triumph of my good grades.

I was the only one in my study group who didn't get admitted anywhere. I was rejected by all seventeen medical schools—with eighteen rejections in all! One school agreed to reevaluate my application but rejected me *again*. I can laugh about it now, but it was pretty stunning.

I didn't know what to do. I'd really wanted this. Was I going to just acknowledge that it wasn't going to happen? I decided to give it three tries. Three was a reasonable number. I was getting older, and in those days, medical schools were favorable neither to women nor to nontraditionally aged students.

My parents doubled down on their initial skepticism. "What do you think you're doing?" they asked. "We have friends who decided to get another career once they had children and a husband and they got divorced. This isn't going to work out for you." But my husband was still—and always has been—very supportive. And the rejections both made me afraid I wasn't going to be able to be a doctor and made me want it more.

I was not a great test taker and hadn't gotten great scores on the MCAT, which is the admissions test. I decided to take a course to improve my scores. By the third try, my scores went to at least an acceptable range. I also went back for additional science courses; my science average was pretty good but was dragged down by a C I'd gotten in college biology.

In the meantime, I got pregnant and had another baby. Now I had a preschooler and an infant. I felt a little like I was torturing everybody around me (especially my husband) by continuing the application process.

Even after so much rejection, it can be overwhelming and confusing to get what you want.

On the day I learned I'd gotten into medical school, I was in tears. I felt like I had to go; I was never going to get this chance again. But I would be leaving my newborn son and my daughter to attend classes every day. At first, I couldn't even tell my parents that I had gotten in.

I spent the summer before medical school trying to learn a little biochemistry, feeling terrified. My son was five months old when school started and my daughter was three and a half. I had had this fantasy that maybe my husband could just stay home and I would go to school, but we wouldn't have had any money, so we hired a babysitter and I did it, an hour-long commute each way.

The first year, students had to take several courses, including anatomy and cell biology. The material was voluminous, and I couldn't believe they expected students to memorize everything. I thought, *Oh, the heart—that's pretty important. But maybe not capillaries?* I failed all three midterms during the first term, each by only a point or two. Looking back, I wonder if I was in some way both obliging and punishing my parents, like, *Think I'm not good enough? You're right!*

To this day, I am eternally grateful to my anatomy professor. He was a lovely former hand surgeon, older, with beautiful white hair and a sort of foreign accent (although I think he was just from Canada). He said, "You have two kids and you're commuting an hour each way! Slow down and take the first year over two years." Nowadays that would be common, but I just thought, *I can't extend this torture.* I told him that I wanted to first see if I could pass the finals and the courses, and he said he'd help me.

I had tutorials with him twice a week before class, just the professor and me and the cadaver. He taught me how to study, saying, "Just read one page. If you learn one thing, that's good. Then read it again—just repeat, repeat, repeat." And that was it. I never failed anything again.

Ultimately, I received my MD and became a psychiatrist. I'm in my seventies and still have a full practice. I think I realized in some way that if you don't get what you want *in the way you want,* you can still have it. You just have to tolerate a different path.

ELIZABETH BELL'S TIPS

TIP 1—When you have a goal, it may not happen in the way you want it to happen. Sometimes you have to have that flexibility to be able to switch modes—to change the path to getting there.

TIP 2—Having supportive study groups made an enormous difference. We relied on one another to learn, but also to share struggles. If you don't need to study, you can still seek out or create groups of supportive peers who meet and help one another deal with work.

MICHELLE TEA

Just because I have some books that are popular or critically acclaimed, it doesn't mean that it's smooth sailing. You risk rejection every time you do anything.

Michelle Tea is a poet, novelist, and performance artist whose work explores queer culture, feminism, and class, among other topics. She has been creating nonstop since she was around twenty. When I spoke with her, she told me that she was living in Los Angeles and in the process of revising a television pilot inspired by one of the pieces in her book *Against Memoir*. She said it was "incredibly hard" to learn a new form, that her natural inclination is "never do an outline, and just write from instinct," but it doesn't work well for a screenplay. Tea also had just pitched an idea for a book to her agent and was revising a young adult novel that she had abandoned several years before for other projects.

Her books include *Valencia, How to Grow Up: A Memoir,* and *Black Wave.* She has published memoirs and novels and edits *Mutha Magazine.* She has multiple nominations and awards, including the PEN/Diamonstein-Spielvogel Award for Art of the Essay.

Lessons I've Learned

*Be bold and say yes to opportunities that come
your way.*

I've always written, but I didn't know that "being a writer" was
an option. Nobody in my family had ever gone to college, and I
didn't go to college either. I moved to San Francisco in my early
twenties, rootless and estranged from my family. It was 1993; I
was writing a lot of poetry, baby dyke love poems or angry, political poems about misogyny or homophobia. There was a big
DIY spoken-word scene influenced by hip-hop and punk and
Bukowski. Anybody could get up and just say what they wanted
to say.

I remember the first time I read out loud and I didn't trust that
my poem was good. It was a little lesbian heartbreak poem read
in "poetry voice," that terrible lilting, dramatic singsong. But my
logic was this: Most things in pop culture had huge followings
even though I personally hated them; I figured *somebody* would
like my poem. In fact, at the end of the night, a little shaved-head
lesbian came over and told me they really liked my poem.

I was like, "Great, I read it for you."

These open mics gave me motivation to keep writing because
I wanted to have new work every night. I also self-published my
poems in chapbooks, which are like zines. But I started wanting
to dive deeper into the experiences I'd written about and began
drafting vignettes that were also meant to be read aloud.

At around this time, Eileen Myles's collection *Chelsea Girls*
came out. I gathered from reading it that they were personal

narratives, and it showed me that writing about your own life sort of counted as literature—maybe someone would even publish it. That was inspiring.

I became kind of obsessed with Eileen. One day, looking through a friend's address book, I saw Eileen's address and phone number and I freaked out. It was like seeing somebody had Beyoncé's information. I was like, "What? How?"

And my friend was like, "Not that big of a deal. Eileen is just a writer like us who walks their dog by my house in New York."

I copied Eileen Myles's address. Then, while on a road trip, I sent a postcard. I was like, *Hey, Eileen. Here I am in Wisconsin. P.S. You don't know me.* Apparently, Eileen was charmed by it and hung it up above their desk.

Months later, I was doing a weekly, all-girl, queer open mic called Sister Spit, and Eileen was coming to town to promote a book. I had their number, so I called and asked if they would read something. Eileen agreed, and I got to host my idol. It was incredible. Eileen went on to write a piece about the Sister Spit open mic for *The Village Voice.* Without my knowledge, Eileen also passed my work around, saying, "This woman should be published." Chris Kraus from Semiotext(e) said, "Okay," and that's how I got my first book.

Meanwhile, I was saying yes to every possible writing opportunity. *The San Francisco Bay Guardian* wanted me to write about "what life's like for dykes in San Francisco right now," and that was really fun. I was like, "Wow. I can't believe I just ran around talking to my friends, wrote about it, and got paid like seven hundred dollars." It was incredible.

Then a lesbian sex magazine called *On Our Backs* had a

column in which writers reported on their sex adventures. I had written about sex in my memoirs and liked taking up the challenge of finding wild things to do and write about. At the time, I wasn't sober, so there was a lot of chemical exploration that dovetailed with sexual exploration. Essentially, the column was sex and drugs and rock and roll. The magazine was a little conflicted about that, but it was the way I wanted to do it.

When someone rejects your creative work, it just means that they can't see a path for it. It doesn't mean there isn't one.

In the nineties, there was a real battle between a radical queer identity and a more assimilationist identity. The privileged white gay men were sort of on top, and then there were the dykes— trans people were barely even discussed, but everybody was kind of marginalized and trying to claw their way into some of the white gay male privilege.

There was a publishing house called Alyson that was the most prominent queer press; to me, it pretty much represented that white gay male prestige.

I had just published a book called *The Passionate Mistakes and Intricate Corruption of One Girl in America,* which had gotten positive attention from *The Nation* and *The Village Voice.* I wrote a proposal for another book, *Valencia,* and was really proud of it. *Valencia* embodied a particular dyke identity, time, and place— an electric, thriving, important culture that was being ignored by mainstream queer culture. I sent the proposal to Alyson Books, feeling pretty confident.

I got a form letter back, rejecting the book. It made me wonder, *Did anyone even read my proposal?*

But I also wondered if my book was too dykey and too outside queer culture. That felt like a political injustice, like they didn't care about this culture, but it also made me feel like more of a little queer outlaw. And in a funny way, it didn't feel totally personal. I never thought it was because my book was bad.

A publishing house called Seal Press went on to publish *Valencia,* and my book won the Lambda Literary Award for Best Lesbian Fiction for that year. At the awards ceremony, the chief editor of Alyson came up to me and said, "So when are you going to write something for Alyson?"

I told him, "I gave you guys *Valencia* and you rejected it." He looked startled. But that was that—it was a very brief exchange.

The experience gave me a lot of perspective: When you imagine a publishing house, it's like this faceless mass of power, but it's probably just one person, especially with midsize or smaller presses. It's one person who likes you or doesn't like you, or even beyond that—maybe it's one person who believes they can market your work or doesn't know how. It's never personal when a publisher or agent doesn't want your book. Even if they don't see a path for it, that doesn't mean there isn't a path for it. They just might not be the person who can forge that path or have those connections or even have that vision.

MICHELLE TEA'S TIPS

TIP 1—If somebody can't publish your book or can't represent you, know that these decisions are all very subjective. It's always literally one or two people who made that decision.

TIP 2—Try not to overidentify with your creative work. It can feel like if somebody doesn't like your work, then they don't like *you*. But your work is this mysterious thing that comes out of you. It's your job to serve it, help it, and then let it go and move on to your next thing.

TIP 3—Finding a creative community will help your work get into the world. A friend passed along the draft of my second book, *Valencia,* to Seal Press. Another book was published by MacAdam/Cage through a writer there who liked me. I feel like everything I've ever gotten has really been through other writers helping me and the literary community.

POLLY RODRIGUEZ

I got three hundred and nine nos before I got my first
yes from an investor. It took two and a half years.

Polly Rodriguez said that when she first started working on
Unbound, a hip website for sex toys and other sexual wellness
products, her mom was "disappointed." It was worse than having
her mom be mad. "She was just like, 'You went from working for
a senator to doing this? What about your reputation? What are
we going to tell the family?' There was so much shame built
into it."

But Rodriguez also realized that doing anything new or socially controversial meant that everyone (not just her mom)
would have an opinion. Male venture capitalists, for example,
sometimes told her, "Well, you know, my wife would *never* use
these products."

No comment on that one.

Rodriguez said that she had to make the decision that the only
people who really mattered were the ones who were using her
products. Early on, customers were e-mailing Unbound to say
how much the company and its products had helped them. "It
was everything from 'I was sexually assaulted in college and being
able to buy these products and reclaim my sexuality changed my
life' to people saying 'I just went through cancer and menopause

and I thought I was the only one, and thank you for taking a stand and talking about this stuff.'"

Under her leadership, Unbound has raised about 3.5 million dollars and has doubled that as the company became profitable, generating about 8 million dollars in revenue.

Lessons I've Learned

Seeing a bunch of mediocre guys run a company made me realize that if they could do it, I could too.

I was diagnosed with cancer at twenty-one, and my doctors said, "There's a thirty percent chance that you'll survive; if you do, there's an eighty percent chance that the cancer will come back." In a way it was liberating. Not knowing how much time I had, I wanted to do the things I'd always dreamed of doing. I became fearless. What did I have to lose?

I'd always wanted to be a politician. I'm from St. Louis and was excited when a Democratic senator, Claire McCaskill, was elected. Barack Obama was in office, and I wanted to work on the Affordable Care Act. It felt personal because I'd lost health insurance after getting cancer and saw how radiation, chemotherapy, and major surgery had almost destroyed my family financially. I got a job working for Senator McCaskill, despite my doctors telling me not to exert myself, and I loved it. However, I became disillusioned by the way in which parts of the ACA were twisted and misinterpreted. For example, when we proposed end-of-life counseling, opponents argued that we wanted to "throw Grandma off a cliff." It was so contentious that I couldn't imagine real change happening.

I worked briefly on Wall Street, but that was soul crushing, and I decided it might be more satisfying to be part of a start-up. In 2014, I joined a group that was developing a dating app. I was one of three female managers and was also leading our launch strategy. All the other women were in operations and customer service. The engineers and CEO were men, and they didn't let women attend product meetings—it was considered "too complex for our skill sets." After team lunches, all the guys would get up and go back to work, expecting the women to clean up. One week I told my team, "We're done cleaning up after these guys. We're not doing it anymore." And then two weeks later, we had a fruit-fly infestation because the dishes just didn't get done. I remember sitting at my laptop, bulk ordering fruit-fly traps, realizing, "I'm fucking done with this."

The experience of seeing how mediocre these guys were, running a company, made me realize: If they can do it, I can too.

I had gotten my hands on a market research report about the sex toy industry and how massive and bad it was. I had some experience with that myself: When I'd been diagnosed with cancer, my doctors hadn't explained that radiation would trigger menopause. At age twenty-one, I found myself shopping for lubricant at a Hustler Hollywood next to the airport—it was the only place that sold that kind of thing in my hometown. It was intimidating and awkward and I remember thinking, *Is this really the best that we can do?*

Through a women-in-tech group, I started talking to a really smart woman who had an idea to start a women's sexual wellness company. We got to talk about how if *we* built a company, it would be different from the other ones out there; body-safe materials, elevated design, educational content that was relatable, and affordable pricing. Walking home that night, I started to panic at the thought of telling my family about our big idea: *Oh my God, I could never be a part of that.* Then I was like: *Why? You own a vibrator. You own lubricant. Why is that your initial reaction?* I also knew that a start-up idea should feel a little scary. If it's not, there are probably a million people already pursuing that idea. Scariness was a sign of potential opportunity. I also wondered: Why is women's sexual well-being taboo when Viagra ads for men are everywhere?

At first, I would go to all these events like "Startup 101" and would watch all these videos. Everybody kept saying, "Start with friends and family as your first round of investors." I was like, "What?" I didn't have friends and family who could write checks, but I started asking literally everybody I knew. It was a mortifying and terrifying experience to just ask people for money.

The first check I got was from my friend Ryan Johnson, with whom I'd grown up in St. Louis. He had sold his Jeep and gave me five thousand dollars. I remember feeling a little overwhelmed by the responsibility and weight of someone giving me that kind of money.

The people rejecting your product might be people who just don't understand it.

I also started applying to every accelerator and every pitch competition, filling out probably ten applications a week. Seventy-five percent of the time, I got rejected on the basis of what we sold. People were just like, "Oh, this is too taboo. This is inappropriate. We couldn't have you come pitch here." What was so hard was the judgment embedded in it. It made me feel like I was doing something dirty or wrong.

There were so many rejections across the board that I started applying to pitch competitions outside New York City. I predicted there would be fewer applicants, and there were; I finally got accepted to a pitch competition in Herndon, Virginia. It was in a crappy hotel ballroom. The guy who got up to pitch right before me was named Darrel and had a manure business. Onstage, he wore these big cowboy boots and talked about fertilizer. I was like, *Great. I literally have to get up right after a pitch about cow shit.* Then I walked onstage and pitched in front of two hundred middle-aged white dudes.

As I started my pitch, which always included my story of going through cancer (because I wanted to explain why our mission was important to me), I was so nervous that my voice shook. And all of a sudden, the men started giggling. Looking back, I realize it was probably because they were uncomfortable, but at the time I thought that they were laughing at me. *They think I'm some stupid little girl,* I thought, *getting up here to pitch my silly business.* It was heartbreaking and embarrassing to have shared a traumatic and vulnerable moment and then to hear people laughing.

But I told myself that I was going to get through it; they were going to hear me out.

At the end there was a Q and A, but no one would ask a question. The organizers started to shoo me offstage so that the next person could pitch. Then, from the back of the room, the only woman in the audience came bursting forward, her hand in the air. She said, "I have a question!" I thought, *Thank God, one person has a question.* And she said, "Can I write you a check right now?"

I just burst into tears. To have this one person believe in me and stand up for me kind of changed everything. She was this incredible professor at Johns Hopkins who said, "I'm going through menopause right now, and this resonates. I understand what you're doing, and I think it's a huge market." Someone was finally taking me seriously and understood what we were trying to do. I got offstage, and she was like, "Here's my card. I will write you a check for five thousand dollars. I will invest."

I went on to raise about 3.5 million dollars in funding and then turned that into more than 8 million dollars in sales, making the company profitable. Not enough people realize that female start-up founders actually return seventy-eight cents to every dollar invested compared to male founders, who return about thirty-one cents to every dollar invested.

I am out fund-raising again right now and am reminded of how painful it is, when you've put your whole life into a company and a vision, to be told that it will never work—over and over and over again. It never stops hurting, even though it does get easier. The most important thing is to just keep going.

POLLY RODRIGUEZ'S TIPS

TIP 1—There is so much power in community, even
if that community includes your competitors. I met a
couple of other female founders who were starting
sex-education-focused businesses, and we became good
friends. I ended up spearheading this organization
called the Women of Sex Tech, which at first was
maybe 5 to 10 female founders, and now it's 250
femme and nonbinary founders.

TIP 2—It's powerful to share experiences of rejection.
We have to be honest with one another about how hard
the process is so that women in business aren't deterred
when it happens to them. I think by sharing your
vulnerability and your hardships, you give other people
permission to do so as well. Then collectively, we're
able to kind of grow stronger together.

LORETTA J. ROSS

Everybody has to deal with oppression, and a few privileged people get paid to fight it.

At Smith, where Professor Loretta J. Ross is a visiting faculty member, there is always a waiting list to get into her course. Ross is a writer, teacher, and activist, the co-founder of the Sister-Song Women of Color Reproductive Justice Collective. "Reproductive justice," a term that Ross actually helped coin, means the right to have power over one's own body, choosing to have children or not, and having the right to raise children in safe communities.

Ross has won numerous awards for her work and has been a guest on *Good Morning America,* BET, and CNN. She has edited, contributed to, and co-authored multiple books. Her most recent book was inspired by "cancel culture," and it's about "calling in" rather than "calling out" when our politics are more alike than different. Calling in includes, for example, welcoming awkward questions with patience and a sense of humor.

"I am what's called a professional feminist," Loretta Ross told me when we sat down in her Smith College office. "I've been an activist since I was a teenager and I'm sixty-six years old now, so you can imagine how long that's been." During our conversation, Ross told me that her activism started because of a lack of sexual autonomy. She was raped as a teenager and kept the baby, but her parents had to sue her local school system to fight for her right to attend her senior year of high school. "That was probably my first act of resistance that could be described as political and feminist," she said, "even though I didn't know anything about either of those two words at the time."

Lessons I've Learned

More experienced women can offer useful advice about being politically smart when your idea is rejected.

I was a mouthy twenty-something-year-old with these baby dreads, dropping "motherfuckers" everywhere, when I was appointed to the DC Commission for Women. These commissions historically were founded so that mayors or governors had somewhere to park the wives of their donors. By definition, commissioners never criticized the person who appointed them—in my case that was Mayor Marion Barry.

Even though the other women on the commission wore gloves and were "ladies" in every sense of the word, they were fierce political advocates, older contemporaries of Dorothy Height and Mary McLeod Bethune. Then I came along, the young director of a rape crisis center—mouthy, bitchy, and feminist. They had every reason not to like me, and I wasn't there to be liked, actually. When DC hit a budget crisis, the city was forced to lay off people and planned on a "last hired, first fired" strategy. I looked at the data, saw a disproportionate number of single black women in the "recently hired" group, and argued that the mayor couldn't take a gender-neutral approach. When the mayor refused to respond to my request for a discussion, the other women on the commission wanted me to just drop it. I was ready to walk past them, slam into his office, and curse him out.

But they had manners. These women, the generations before me, were good at being cunning with kindness. One of them took me outside of the meeting and said, "You have a seat at the table, and maybe you think it's your job to turn the table over. But don't forget who opened the door for you to get that seat in the first place. I don't need you being impertinent to us."

And she was right. They weren't my enemies, but I was treating them as such because they didn't move as fast as I thought they should move, or in the way that I thought they should move.

There can be a lesson in a rejection: I should have slowed down and brought my boss into the conversation before making a decision.

During the 1980s, I mobilized women of color for reproductive rights, directing the women-of-color program for NOW, organizing marches and campaigns for the protection of abortion rights. By 1989, I was one of the leading black abortion rights activists in the country and was recruited by the founder of the National Black Women's Health Project. Byllye Avery wanted me as her program director.

Now Byllye was a rock star and still is one of my rock stars. She had organized the first national conference on black women's health in 1983 and co-founded an abortion clinic and a birthing center, both in Florida. I didn't think twice about the decision to pick up my life and move from Washington, DC, to Atlanta to be on her staff. She was a mentor and someone whom I knew I would learn from. But I'll always remember that one of the first things she said to me was, "Loretta, if you don't keep my secrets, I'm going to have to fire you."

I was second-in-command, and within a year and a half, Byllye had another job open. She was hiring someone to run our international program and swore me to secrecy about whom she had selected. I wouldn't have any problem keeping her secret, I thought. And then one of the candidates called me.

This candidate told me that she had been offered her dream job, a chance to be on the editorial board of *The Atlanta Journal-Constitution*. She would turn it down if she was truly in the running for the international program job at the National Black Women's Health Project. I knew that she was not Byllye's chosen candidate, and I thought, *Our decision has been made, just not announced*. I told her, "You'd better go take that job."

But no good deed goes unpunished. The candidate called Byllye right away to tell her she was withdrawing her name from our search and, during that call, revealed that I'd told her she was no longer in the running.

Byllye invited me to her home for dinner. She really is a wonderful person and wanted to break the news to me in her home.

"Loretta," she said, "if I can't count on you to keep my secrets, I'm going to have to fire you."

I was crushed. "Wait a minute," I said. "You're firing me for telling the truth?" It just didn't seem logical to me. Why would we block this candidate, who we knew damn well wasn't getting the job, from becoming one of the first black women to get a position at *The Atlanta Journal-Constitution*? I thought Byllye would agree with my logic, and when she didn't, I yelled about how wrong she was. I was hurt, disappointed, and angry.

I was also in shock because I didn't know what I was going to do next. To take a job with her, I had quit a previous job and moved to a new city.

This was an emotional time for me personally but also for the reproductive justice movement. A tribute conference was planned in Boston for the poet and feminist activist Audre Lorde, who was in the last stages of cancer. I had planned to fly there but instead decided to just point my Toyota from Atlanta toward Boston and go. Two girlfriends from Georgia came along, and we picked up a third in DC.

Traveling to the conference, and once we arrived, I told the story to those friends and to others who knew both me and Byllye. It was complicated because I still loved her and we were part of the same movement, working toward goals that were deeply important to me. In the end, the job with Byllye was just a job, but we knew we were going to continue to engage with each other.

Though I was as angry as hell, I started to see her point of view. She had explicitly told me, "If you don't keep my secrets, I'm going to fire you"; no ambiguity there. But I was young and self-righteous and thought telling the truth should triumph over every other commitment that a person makes. How naïve. In retrospect, I see now that I could've *asked* Byllye what she thought we should do. I didn't have to take this on alone! My consulting her would've created a win-win for all of us, because it would have shown that I understood the necessity for loyalty. I hadn't wanted to hurt Byllye, but the fact was, I hadn't brought the problem to her to solve. I had violated her confidence and she was right to call me on that.

In Boston, we met with Audre and celebrated her life, and it put things in perspective. I was fortunate to have that black feminist community coming from around the country. It was healing, even though it was also about loss. Months later, Audre was gone.

By the time I got back to Atlanta, I'd gotten a job offer to become program director at the Center for Democratic Renewal (formerly National Anti-Klan Network). Five years with them led to deeper anti-fascism work, and today I teach about white supremacy at colleges all over the United States.

As for Byllye, she had this capacity to almost effortlessly make people love her. It was born out of a genuine caring for people and an emotional intelligence. I mean, I could get so angry at her and I still couldn't stop loving her. We remained friends in part because she's so lovable, but in part because I took time to reflect on what had happened; I was mature enough to see what I had done to cause the break in our working relationship.

LORETTA J. ROSS'S TIPS

TIP 1—Do the work you want to do and then find a way to get paid to do it. Sometimes that means finding the organization that most aligns with what you want to do and volunteering there, or working your way up the food chain, or writing or blogging so that you become a self-taught expert.

TIP 2—If you care enough about your work, you will be able to get past rejections. Even after I was fired, my former boss and I knew that we were in the same movement. Our relationship changed, but we were still part of the black feminist community working for reproductive justice.

TIP 3—It's almost too cliché, but often when one door closes, another one opens. That's exactly what happened to me.

ALYSIA REINER

Over the course of my career, I have been on thousands of auditions. Ninety percent of them I didn't get. The funny thing is that getting ten percent is actually really good odds!

Alysia Reiner was my first interview for this book, and as soon as our phone interview was over, I realized that my recording equipment hadn't been working. I scrambled to type as much of the interview as I could remember and wrote a thank-you to Alysia, too embarrassed to reveal my screw-up (even though I'd edited an entire book on work mistakes). As my deadline got closer, I decided to just e-mail her and admit what had happened. She was completely understanding and agreed right away to a do-over.

Alysia has been going to professional auditions since high school, when her acting teacher got a call for kids to try out for *Dead Poets Society,* a 1989 movie directed by Peter Weir and starring Robin Williams. The director watched her audition and gave her immediate feedback that she never forgot: "I'm not giving you this part," he said, "because you look about thirty and the character is supposed to be a child. But I do want to tell you that you're a very good actress and should continue with this." He wasn't finished. "Now," he continued, "people will tell you to get a nose job. Don't do it. Your nose suits your face and you have a fabulous profile. There are a few tricky angles, but if cinematography knows how to film your face correctly, it's not a problem."

He was referring to Alysia's Mediterranean-looking nose, a nose that fits perfectly on her beautiful face so that she looks like she's right out of a painting by Modigliani. For the next fifteen years that nose, deemed "exotic" by the powers that be, along with the fact that she looked older than her years, meant that her success was not mainstream. Reiner was in off-Broadway plays and in commercials, and she won acclaim in a one-woman show about Virginia Woolf at the Edinburgh Festival in Scotland. Meanwhile, during the early years of her career, both strangers and relatives offered to purchase a nose job for her. She declined.

At a certain point, Alysia had enough success that she secured an agent, who sent her the script for *Orange Is the New Black,* a pilot for one of the first Netflix shows. It took multiple auditions to secure the role of Fig, for which she won a Screen Actors Guild Award. She also plays Pamela Adlon's best friend, Sunny, in all four seasons of FX's Peabody Award–winning *Better Things* and recently joined the cast of HBO's critically acclaimed *The Deuce* for seasons two and three. Additionally she has guest starred and had recurring roles on some cult favorite shows like *How to Get Away with Murder, Broad City, Odd Mom Out,* and *Masters of Sex.* She lives in New York City with her husband and daughter.

Lessons I've Learned

I'm always auditioning and so in a sense always waiting to hear back about jobs; it has helped to be of service to the planet and also to be creative—to make my own work.

When my agent sent me the script for *Orange Is the New Black,* I thought it was brilliant. It was based on a memoir by Piper Kerman, a Smith College graduate who, as a young woman, agreed to help a drug-dealing girlfriend with a transport mission across international borders and went to jail for it. I originally auditioned to play Alex, one of the lead roles. Before I went into the audition, the casting director warned me: "Jenji Kohan doesn't like to talk and neither does Michael, the other producer who'll be in the room. So don't talk directly to them."

For the audition, they had me read a few scenes from the pilot. One was in the past, when Alex was falling in love; another was in the present, in prison. A good audition feels like you're fully present, not just saying lines but engaged in a conversation. You're in it, not watching yourself, and there's this magic that happens when you're in the zone, so that even if you drop a line you can pick it up and keep going. That's what my audition felt like, but while it was happening, Jenji didn't say a word, and Michael didn't even look at me.

Then it was over. I felt so good about what had just happened that before I left the room, I decided I was going to break the rules. "I just need to say," I told Jenji, "this script is so good. I know everybody loves *Weeds* [a show Jenji created] and I'm sure you hear that often. But you also wrote on one of my favorite shows of all time, *The Tracey Ullman Show,* and that actually inspired me to keep acting."

Jenji lit up and started chatting. "That was one of my favorite jobs ever!" she said. "It was the best writers' room because it was run by a woman and incredibly civil. We left at a decent hour every day [which a lot of writers' rooms don't] and after the show on Thursdays we would all drink red wine."

I responded, "Well, when I get this job, I'll bring a bottle of red wine every Thursday." It was so unlike me, but standing there talking to her, I felt that confident.

Then I left and didn't hear anything. When you're an actor, you learn how to feel awesome and blow an audition out of the water and then just let it go, because you have so little power over the process of being cast. Learning to let it go is as much a part of your craft as anything. I advise beginning actors to make a plan for every day. Ideally, it should include at least one experience that feeds one's "inner artist"—going to a museum or a movie or reading a book of poetry or painting something, creating something—and one that relates to the business of being an artist: reading a script, doing a staged reading, sending a mailing to potential agents, going to a networking event, meeting with a director. Having a plan each day keeps me productive and levelheaded. For me this also has morphed into producing my own work.

I also encourage beginning actors to try to be of service to the planet whether they get jobs or not. Activism in my New York City neighborhood keeps me feeling connected to the community and brings me a lot of joy. I'm part of an amazing organization called Action Potluck, which helps to organize resources for local refugees. I also work with formerly incarcerated people and do a lot of work with Time's Up.

Sometimes "no" is just "not this and not yet."

So I kept myself busy and kept auditioning. A couple of months after that first audition for the role of Alex, I got an audition to play another main character, Polly, Piper's best friend. *Ah,* I thought. *I didn't get Alex because I'm supposed to play Polly. That's what it is!* Again I went in, loved the role, and thought I did a great scene. But again, I didn't get it.

Another month went by. One day, out of the blue I got a phone call. "They want to offer you the role of Fig on *Orange Is the New Black,*" said my agent. Fig was the assistant to the prison warden. It would be recurring, he told me, but at the time, Fig had only three lines. Still, I remember my excitement as I stood in my living room with my two-year-old daughter. After I hung up, we danced around the sofa, jumping up and down. I was so excited. Incredibly, Fig evolved from three lines into a fleshed-out seven-year role with an incredible arc. I have since heard that Jenji knew right away that I wasn't right for Alex but also knew that she wanted to put me somewhere in the show. That was the biggest compliment ever!

An acting coach once told me that the great thing about an audition is that you get to do the scene your way. Even if you don't get the job, it's yours during the audition—for those three minutes. I auditioned for something just yesterday, a new secret project for HBO with some fancy director. I worked really hard and it felt good but I don't know what's going to happen. Still, I can let it go because I didn't leave thinking, *I wish I had done it differently.*

ALYSIA REINER'S TIPS

TIP 1—Reframe auditions as opportunities to work and to network. Every job interview, every time you read for a role, it is a chance to do the work that you love and to meet new people—writers, showrunners, casting directors—and have them meet you.

TIP 2—If you can't find a mentor, then create a mentorship group of friends where you all cheer one another on and hold one another accountable.

ALLY EINBINDER

Learning how to be a working artist or working musician is almost one hundred percent learning through mistakes and difficult experiences. It's enticing to see dollar signs and to have enthusiastic people speaking about your band in a way that's bigger than you ever imagined. You're flung into this professional role before you realize, "Oh, this is a job, and I can choose who I work with."

Ally Einbinder is the bassist in the band Potty Mouth. She grew up in Albany, New York, and attended Smith College, where she majored in sociology. As she prepared for graduation, Ally was offered a prestigious fellowship to attend graduate school. Her professors thought she had the talent and drive to become an academic, but Ally wanted something else. She told me, "Music is the thing in my life that makes me feel the most alive, specifically performing and playing with other people. It wasn't until I heard myself play bass with a whole band and a whole group of people that I began to realize how powerful that is." She also loves touring and playing shows, seeing other parts of the world, meeting people, and being an example for young women. "I definitely didn't have that growing up," she said. "I grew up going to punk shows and I almost never, ever saw women perform." Since their debut album came out in 2013, Potty Mouth has released an EP on Atlantic Records, played at Lollapalooza and at Radio City Music Hall, and appeared on *Last Call with Carson Daly*. They have played shows with the Scottish band Chvrches and the Go-Go's. Their second album, *Snafu,* came out in 2019.

Lessons I've Learned

Small goals are good: You can start a band just by having fun playing instruments. It's also exciting to let your goals get bigger and bigger.

Growing up in Albany, I was always into music but was never in a band. A lot of my male friends were in bands, and it seemed so easy for them. I would watch one of them just pick up a guitar, start playing something, and be like, "I've never taken a lesson. I just know how to do this."

In 2011, a year out of college, I started playing bass and practicing with my friend's band, Outdates. Having graduated from Smith, a women's college, I realized how powerful it was to be in classrooms with mostly women; it built my confidence. I wanted to see what it would be like to be in a band with other women who, like me, were just starting.

I knew Victoria, our drummer, because she went to Smith. I knew Phoebe, our original guitarist, from Smith. And Abby is also from the area, from Amherst. We didn't have big expectations; we wanted to just get together, jam, and see what happened.

We started out playing in my house, usually in the basement, and set a couple of small goals. I had watched so many of my friends starting bands, putting out records, and touring, that I knew it was possible. You can book yourself a tour to New York and Boston and Philly. You don't have to go that far. I was like, "I would be content if we released at least a four-song EP and did a short tour around it."

When we released that first EP, we sent it to music blogs and people started reviewing it. Soon we were playing as much as possible, just saying yes to everything—I remember there was one month where I had a show every weekend. We were self-promoting, which helped. We just wanted people to hear our music.

Then our goals kept getting bigger. A big label in the UK happened to hear our EP because someone in their office was playing it. The label, Rough Trade, reached out to us over e-mail and said they wanted to hear more demos. That was when we started to realize the potential in the band. People were noticing us and thought what we were doing was good and legitimate, and our goals just became bigger.

In 2014, we got a development deal with Atlantic Records. It was exciting to get all this money from a major label. We used the money to put out a five-song EP in 2015, and even though Atlantic ended up dropping us, we decided to move from Western Massachusetts to Los Angeles. It was a big decision, but it felt like an investment in the band.

*Sometimes it's worth pushing back on a rejection to
get what you need in order to move on.*

We moved to LA in 2016, and our manager was eager to pass us
on to his friend Jack,* who was just starting a new management
company. We were one of the first bands on their roster. Jack and
Sam were celebrities who had been musicians themselves. When
they had started out, they'd been thrown into a major label
deal and hadn't known how to navigate it; now they wanted to
guide and nurture early-stage artists. Their fancy glass-walled
office was filled with high-end equipment, and they had an in-
house recording studio, engineer, and creative team. They were
like, "You can record your album here for free using all of our
resources. We can make music videos for you." It was comforting
to think: *Here are these rich, famous people who think what we're
doing is cool, and they're also like a family—they're going to help
take care of us.*

For example, once we had money to buy a van, they encouraged us, saying, "Listen, you need to be on the road and you
need a van to tour in." Then they helped us find one that was
affordable. Another example: Their intern went and looked at
LA apartments for us while we were on tour. He even did a video
of an apartment and sent it to me and Abby. I was like, "Wow,
this must be what it's like to be a celebrity. You just have people
looking for apartments for you." Because I had no income at the
time, no pay slips to show a potential landlord, the management
company wrote me a reference.

---

* Names in this section of Ally's story have been changed.

We stayed with that company for two years, and there were good parts of the relationship. They were accessible and made us feel like we could reach out anytime we had a question or wanted to talk. They were good at helping us figure out how to do things on a budget, which also meant leaning heavily on in-house resources. We got to use their studio and engineer to record most of our album, something we'd never be able to afford otherwise. Their creative team made two music videos for us, and the company hooked us up with brand partnerships, so we got a lot of freebies—mostly shoes, clothes, and sometimes guitars and amps.

In the music industry, there's all this talk about developing bands, figuring out how to brand them, all this time spent on image and looks. I think Jack and Sam thought we already had that, which was cool. I don't want anyone to change us. The problem was that they thought our image *alone* was going to propel us forward. They saw us as these cool girls rolling in as our own prepackaged thing, meanwhile giving them this cool, indie rock credibility. They thought that once we started working with them, record labels were going to come knocking on their door.

No record labels came knocking. Jack and Sam didn't know how to market us. They passed us through five or six different day-to-day managers, but as time went on, it felt like they weren't even listening to anything that we were doing in the studio. We would send stuff and they would never respond. In meetings, we would play them a song we wrote, and they would be like, "Yeah, it's good, but we really need a song like *this*." And you could just hear what was guiding their ideas about "this" kind of song. It was about a formula for what worked on the radio: "An album should have a song that's this many beats per minute, because you can't just have an album of songs that are all mid-tempo, you need to have a fast one." They thought their formula was the key to making a good record and always seemed to think there was something missing from what we were doing.

It started to feel scary because initially, there had been a plan that we would make an album by a certain date. Then that date would come, and our time in the studio would get pushed back. Other bands that had been signed to labels, with budgets to pay for their studio time, got to record instead.

We would go in the studio for these short bursts, lay down some tracks, and wouldn't be in there again for months. Something would be eighty percent done and we wouldn't know when we'd be able to go back in. Making music this way took the steam out of everything.

Finally, in February of 2018, we went to their office to advocate for ourselves, to say, "We need to finish our album."

I remember sitting at the table as the company's general manager smiled like he had a great idea. "What if we do a Kickstarter," he said, "to get you girls some money to finish the album? We can tie it to the 'It's Me' campaign!"

We were like, "What are you talking about?"

"You know," he pressed. "You'll do a Kickstarter and make it an 'It's Me' thing?" This was right when women in the entertainment industry were coming out and telling their stories of working with terrible men or being sexually assaulted—and it turned out he was talking about the #MeToo movement.

Victoria started laughing. I thought, *Are you serious? Do you even understand what you're saying right now? Are you really telling a bunch of women to finance their album—something we were sup-posed to make* for free in your studio—*through Kickstarter and saying what?* "Hey, yeah. We've all been sexually assaulted. Give us money. We've all had these horrible experiences. It's MeToo. Give us money for our album." It was insane.

But we left that meeting with a plan: The management com-pany agreed to put time on the calendar, saying, "We'll give you two weeks to finish your album."

"That's totally doable," we said, and set a studio date.

Then things got worse. Soon after that meeting, we got an e-mail from Jack and Sam's older brother. It was a Sunday and he wrote, "Hey, girls. Can we get on the phone tomorrow to have a catch-up call?"

On Monday, we got on a conference call, and the first thing he said was: "As of today, our company can no longer represent you." We hadn't finished the album and they wanted us out of there. He added, "The good news is you can have the raw tracks of everything you've worked on!"

That was not good news. There was no way to take those raw tracks, give them to another producer, and ask, "Can you help us finish this?" Musicians don't work that way. The studio and the equipment were so specific.

We got off the phone feeling angry, like they had totally fucked us over. We had sacrificed a lot over two years working on that album. Abby had deferred college. I had moved far from my fam-ily and everyone I love. We had put so much on the line because we trusted them, and it felt like getting dumped by family.

When we gave the news to the producer who had been hired

by their company to make our album, he was mad. He told us, "This is something I've been working on too. I love this album. I want to see it done."

We went back to Jack and Sam and used our anger to power a new round of negotiations, and they agreed to let us finish it in their studio, with the same producer, with all the tracking and editing—but we had to do it over two days, rapid-fire. And it wasn't over. They tried to get money from us, saying, "Over the course of our relationship, we invested over thirty thousand dollars in you girls." It was always *you girls*. "We know our relationship meant something to you," they said, "and we'd hope that you'd find it in your heart to throw us what you can."

Abby got on the phone with Jack and said, "Of course we are so appreciative of everything you've done and for believing in us, but we put a lot of trust in your company. The money we have, we have to live off of. There's no extra." He backed off.

But the experience felt awful. In music you need a reason to believe in yourself; otherwise it can feel like a vanity project. Having people from outside being like, "There's potential here, this doesn't have to be a Bandcamp project—it could be your life," who doesn't want that? Once they stopped thinking we were special, it made me wonder: *Does this mean we've failed?*

But we moved on. In two days, we finished the album. We paid for the mixing ourselves and released it on our own terms.

As a band, it's easy to surrender yourself to this idea that you need a team of people managing you—and that is not always the case.

Everyone in the music industry has an idea about what's best for you, and because you become fatigued by all the decisions, it's easy to rely on a management company to make them. However, the more labor we passed on, the less in control we were. Soon after we left the company, we learned that the new representative from our publishing company had been trying to introduce herself and say she had free studio space for us to write and record in. She showed us forty e-mails that had never been forwarded. If we had known, we could have tried to finish our album sooner and on our own terms.

I'm proud that we figured out how to get the album done, release it, and create a marketing campaign within a year of being dropped by Jack and Sam. We had built relationships with other people in the music business, and they've stuck with us. For example, our publicist has been doing our press since our 2015 EP with Atlantic, and she's become like a sister to us.

After the album came out, *LA Weekly* called us the best punk band in LA. It's hard to make a name for yourself out here and it's nice to be acknowledged as an LA band. As an artist, the ultimate goal is to get to the point where you're only working on the music—not doing your own booking or marketing, your own e-mails or business management. Who wouldn't want to *just* be creative and musical? That's the fun part about being in a band. The rest of it isn't really that fun. But for now, we're going back to our roots, promoting ourselves and being our own powerhouse team. It led us to success when we were starting out, and it's working again. None of us come from families with any background in the music industry, so all we have is our ability to reflect on our experiences and use that to inform our decisions as we navigate relationships and deals.

Despite some hard times, playing music is still the only thing in the world that makes all my anxiety go away. I've never found anything else like that. Just playing music with other people is the only thing that makes every other thought temporarily stop.

ALLY EINBINDER'S TIPS

TIP 1—It's easy to get used to having someone else just tell you the right way to do things, but there's a difference between *needing* a team and *wanting* the comfort.

TIP 2—A band is like a group project. You're taking four different people with four different lives and somehow trying to make it work together. It's important to have conversations like, "How much of our lives do we want to commit to this?"

PART 3

Rejection Is a Muscle

It was the weekend before her dissertation defense, and environmental social scientist Caitlin Kirby sat at her computer, searching her e-mail for the word "unfortunately." She was looking for rejection letters, especially long ones—those were the most aesthetically pleasing. Caitlin was going to make a skirt out of rejection letters, crafting it from tulle and paper, and she planned to wear this skirt to her dissertation defense at Michigan State University.

"I'm not normally doing crafts all weekend," Caitlin told me, "but I wanted to make a statement about how getting a doctorate is a marathon, not a sprint. I wanted to speak to the journey and normalize rejection as part of the process."

She remembers her first rejections most vividly: the first National Science Foundation fellowship rejection; the first journal article rejection; the first conference presentation rejection. "After that," Caitlin said, "they're all a little fuzzier; they fade into the background." In a certain way, she thinks rejection tolerance is like a muscle—she bears disappointment with increasing strength, and rejections have felt easier over time. But just as muscles hurt after a new exercise, rejection after a new risk can be painful. "It can still hit hard when you get the first one," Caitlin said.

Okay—how did Caitlin Kirby become the kind of kick-ass scientist who wears an outfit made out of rejection letters to her dissertation defense? She told me that every week, her advisor, Julie Libarkin, convened a group of graduate students, postdocs, and professors. They were invited to share accomplishments but also to talk about a rejection or failure from the week—a grant or paper turned down, a deadline not met. "These meetings," Caitlin told me, "helped to normalize rejection and failure, especially for the younger students, so that nobody would feel they weren't 'good enough' to be in that space." Over time, it got easier for Caitlin to share her rejections too.

She had seen other doctoral candidates post pictures of dresses made from their presentation posters; she had also watched a *Parks and Rec* episode in which main character Leslie Knope gets married in a dress made of flyers and news clippings from her career in the parks department.

On the day that Caitlin put on her rejection skirt and wore it to her talk, she got a lot of curious stares but also heard from the graduate students in attendance that the skirt was comforting. "They really appreciated it as far as not feeling anxious about their own failures," said Caitlin. "And I know some of the professors or lab PIs [principal investigators] took pictures to share with their labs."

By the time we spoke, Caitlin had graduated from her doctoral program, was wrapping up a Fulbright Fellowship, and was preparing for a postdoctoral position at the University of Nebraska–

Lincoln. She'd had a lot of success. But she told me, "It still sucks to get rejected. I'm not immune to it now."

How does she deal with it? She allows herself to be upset initially "because that's a totally normal reaction." After a bit of time, she goes back and tries to think about what she did well. "If I'm at a place where I think it's useful," she said, "then I might think about things that I could do better." When addressing comments in a rejected journal article, "even though I don't initially enjoy it," she told me that she usually feels better after putting in the work. She also knows that "a lot of times rejection or failure is up to chance—right place, right time—and not really a reflection of how well you did."

In the upcoming section, interviewees talk about getting rejected over and over and getting pretty good at dealing with it. Comedian Sam Jay told me about starting comedy after the age of thirty and bombing during her first time onstage. People booed her. (Seriously. Imagine being booed. Ugh.) She brushed it off because she knew what she wanted and that she would need to get up onstage *a lot*. Writer Emily Winter spent a year aiming for one hundred rejections; Kate Manne, the philosopher, tells her students to try for fifty: As soon as a rejected article comes back, another goes out.

Dealing with rejection can strengthen you. That doesn't mean it stops being painful. It doesn't mean you'll want to make clothing out of your rejection letters. (Who knows, though? Maybe you will!) It does mean that you'll get better at dealing with it.

KERI SMITH

I have a manuscript that is sitting with my publisher. I submitted something that they did not expect and I have no idea if they'll like it; I could be crushed tomorrow. Waiting is nail-biting. At the same time, I personally like the manuscript. And I know I'll be okay because I have a lot of practice going through failure in small ways. That has led me to an acceptance of bigger things too.

The artist and writer Keri Smith, bestselling author of *Wreck This Journal* and *How to Be an Explorer of the World,* along with more than a dozen other books, is extremely humble for someone who's kind of famous. Her humility was evident throughout our conversation, and especially in a vignette she told me as we were wrapping up.

Keri spends a lot of time reading and "making connections between different things that shouldn't be connected," so she needs access to libraries. When she moved to Northampton, she was excited to visit the Smith College library. However, she also has a constant nagging worry about not belonging in academic spaces. Anytime she enters an academic library, she says, "I always have this baggage where I don't feel like I'm allowed to be there."

Soon after moving, Keri biked over to the Smith College library to find out if she'd be able to borrow our books, even though she didn't work at the college. The young woman working at the desk said she would need to talk to her boss and asked to see a driver's license. When she looked at the license, she gasped. "Are you Keri Smith the writer?"

Smith told me, "I was like, 'Well, yeah, I think . . . I don't know if I'm the same one you're thinking.'"

The woman at the desk said, "Oh my God, I'm such a huge fan of yours!" And this made Keri Smith happy, not specifically because the woman knew her name, but because "every time I would go in there, she'd be like, 'Can I help you find stuff?'"

Keri's humility, creativity, and curiosity about the world, along with her willingness—almost a determination—to make mistakes, all contribute to her work. Talking to her about it was a lot of fun.

Lessons I've Learned

Practice allowing yourself to not be perfect.

I attended public school in Canada and did not do well academically. I procrastinated on everything, starting papers and not finishing them, telling myself that it wasn't worth it because the final product wouldn't be perfect. I was also really disorganized. These days, kids can get diagnosed with "executive functioning" issues and then get some help, but I never had any help, and it was a mess for me.

My family life was also difficult. When I was in high school, my mom became terminally ill, so I was dealing with that—but not really dealing with it. No one had the bandwidth to pay attention to anything I was doing, and I didn't feel like anyone at school cared about me.

By grade twelve, I was failing everything. But one day, one of my teachers asked me to come to his office. When I got there, he told me to sit down. Then he asked, "What are you doing with your life? What are you interested in?"

Nobody had ever asked me that. I told him that I kind of liked to draw. He responded, "Okay, come back tomorrow and bring me some drawings that you've done."

The next day, I returned with my drawings. My teacher looked through them and was quiet. Then he said. "Out of all the students in your graduating class, you will be the one to succeed."

I thought, *He must be crazy,* and told him he was wrong. But the teacher continued, saying I knew how to think for myself, that this was important. The teacher suggested that I apply to art school for college, but I knew that I wasn't even going to graduate high school. There was no way.

When high school was over, I got a job at a bookstore and decided that I was just going to read all the books that my friends were being assigned at university. Part of me didn't think I was smart enough, but another part had this curiosity. I wanted to see if I could handle college-level reading. *Could I do it?*

My best friend shared her syllabus, and I plowed through every book, becoming increasingly excited because I realized, "Oh, I can totally do this. I understand these books." For the first time, I realized that maybe I *was* smart.

I loved working in the bookstore and stayed there for two years. During that time, another of my high school teachers came in. When he saw me working there, he asked, "You're going to work in a bookstore for the rest of your life?" I actually loved my job, but the question sparked a new determination. If someone tells me I can't, then I rebel. I did some research on how I *could* go to college if I wanted to. I found a loophole in the Canadian system that allowed me to apply as a "mature student."

I was accepted at the Ontario College of Art with a focus on illustration, and once I was there, my life opened up. I was learning every day, hungry for it—the chance to be challenged and to experiment and play—and I graduated.

During my early years as a commercial illustrator, I wished that I could write and illustrate my own stuff, but I didn't have confidence. Instead, I created a space to do work just for me, a beautiful, safe place where I journaled, using collage and writing, spewing it all into one space. All my flaws—procrastination, fear of starting—led to a daily question: *What's the bare minimum I can do to feel some sense of accomplishment?* Maybe it was just getting a mark on the page. Or destroying something. I went through my journal, one page at a time.

Working at the bookstore, I had always been drawn to the quirky books near the cash register, the ones that couldn't be categorized on shelves. And I had met people who worked in publishing. At a certain point, I wondered whether my journal work could become one of those quirky books. That's how *Wreck This Journal* was born.

Experiments are not really encouraged in our culture, and my work ended up being about helping me—and others—do experiments and create failure in small ways. Making mistakes on purpose habituates you, making you more comfortable with not being perfect.

You don't need to pay attention to every critique, and you don't need to be good at everything.

But some people are really triggered by the idea of failing on purpose. There's something about my work that really pushes people into a place where they're mad and angry with me, and I've literally gotten hate mail about it.

It's hard not to be hurt by a mean letter or comment on the internet, because every time I do a book, I've put my whole self into it. It's intimate. When people are mean in a vitriolic way about my work, it can feel brutal; there's no way around it. I used to go to my husband and say, "You can't believe what people have been saying to me!"

He would respond, "You don't even know those people. Why do you care what they think?" That was a good point: Why do I care about those people when I don't even know them? Even with a bad review, I don't have to care what the reviewer thinks.

One of my worst moments of rejection was at an academic conference at Johns Hopkins in Baltimore. I was on a panel called "Learning, Arts and the Brain" and had been flattered to be asked.

I spoke about the merging of the creative and scientific mind and challenged the audience to engage in what Einstein called "thought experiments." Then one of my co-panelists, a psychologist from Harvard, started to argue with me: "You can't use

Einstein as an example!" he said. "Einstein was an anomaly! Average people cannot do thought experiments and have them succeed!"

He was animated in his attempt to tear me down, and I became flustered and intimidated. I felt the return of my very old shame—from back in high school!—about not being "academic" enough. That panel was more than ten years ago, but if the same thing happened now, I would probably tell myself: *I never went to graduate school, but why can't my education, and my self-learning, be valid?*

These days, I have more confidence and more self-compassion. I am also less perfectionistic than I used to be. I recently joined a singing group because I love to sing. After our first session, this other woman around my age, also new to the group, whispered to me, "Oh God, I just feel like the teacher's really harsh and I'm worried that I'm not singing well."

I said to her, "I have all of those thoughts too, but I finally feel like I really don't give a shit. If I'm not singing well, I'm going to come every week, I'm going to do my best. Because I enjoy it and I don't need to be really good at it." I do think that's because of all my years of preparation. I'm willing to not be great. I'm willing to experience failure.

KERI SMITH'S TIPS

TIP 1—It's important to practice failing by participating in things where your chance of failing is high. I started sewing when I was in high school. When you begin sewing, you're guaranteed to make clothes that you do not want to wear. But when you push yourself to tolerate failure over and over, you're not as crushed by it.

TIP 2—We have commodified our leisure time on Instagram, so it's, "I'm going to take a photo of myself doing this thing," and your life becomes about getting likes. I believe we need to reclaim private space for contemplation, for doing something just for ourselves, to not show anybody else.

EMILY WINTER

In comedy and entertainment, you can put eighty hours of work into something, send it out, and not hear back. You're *lucky* to hear a no. And you can't convince yourself that it didn't matter; you just spent eighty hours on it! In other parts of society, that kind of behavior—to take somebody's eighty hours of work and ignore it—would be preposterous. It's really hard, and that is why I have so many projects going all the time.

You may have heard Emily Winter's jokes on NPR's *Ask Me Another* or read one of her hilarious "Shouts & Murmurs" pieces in *The New Yorker,* or maybe you saw her on the *Today* show talking about her project of collecting one hundred rejections—more on that later in this chapter.

Emily Winter writes and performs stand-up but also regularly produces several successful comedy events on the side. She said that learning to produce felt intuitive: "I think that's a gender thing, because women are taught to facilitate other people enjoying themselves and to be attuned to other people's moods and needs. All of those skills helped me in producing." She created a thirty-two-city festival in 2017 during Trump's inauguration weekend, raising fifty thousand dollars for the ACLU. With a friend, she produces and hosts a one-liner, single-elimination joke contest each year at the Bell House in Brooklyn and has taken that show all over the country. In addition to her stand-up and producing gigs and her writing job at *Ask Me Another,* Winter is working on multiple pilots and a screenplay with her comedian/writer husband, Chris Calogero.

Lessons I've Learned

A rejection can feel like it was your "one shot at success and fulfillment." That doesn't mean that it is.

When a TV show needs a writer, they tell their staff and reach out to agents and managers. If you don't know anyone on staff or you don't have an agent or manager, you will not find out. There's no other way. They don't post on Indeed or anything. Once you're allowed to apply, you get a writing assignment that's called a "packet." It's usually about three to five pages of specific writing prompts, from monologue jokes to topical sketches, desk bits or field pieces.

In 2017, I got a packet for *The Daily Show* through a friend who works there. These things take forever. You throw yourself into them. You don't shower. You put off other deadlines. You don't go to work. Doing a packet is all-consuming.

After submitting it, I got a call saying that they wanted me to do a follow-up, a *round two* packet! I was like, "Oh my God! You guys want me to do another one!" I did the second one, and then I got an interview at *The Daily Show*. I was so excited and so nervous. I went in and met Trevor Noah. I met the executive producers. They were very complimentary about my writing. And then I didn't get the job.

I found out via social media, which is pretty standard. Usually, you don't find out until somebody posts a picture of themselves at what would be your desk, saying, "Oh, it's my first day here!"

In my case, I was on Facebook chatting with a friend who was a writer at *Last Week Tonight,* and he mentioned two former *LWT* writers were up for a job at *The Daily Show.*

I was like, "Noooo! *I'm* up for a job at *The Daily Show!*" I thought, *I can't compete with a writing pair that just came from* Last Week Tonight. *I don't have that kind of résumé.* And it turned out they did get the *Daily Show* positions. I was just like, "I have no more to give. That was everything."

I remember sitting at my desk in my little home office. I already had figured it out by the time I got an e-mail from Comedy Central, but I was still crushed. That was my shot and I didn't get it.

It sounds strange, but aiming for rejection can lead to success.

I have this star chart in my office, literally a teacher's incentive chart that you can buy. I give myself a star after every twenty minutes of writing, and I wondered, *What if I began tracking my rejections?* I had seen an article about some poet who got fifty rejections in a year. I thought, *If a poet is getting fifty, a comedian should be able to get double that because poetry is slow.* Poets are working six weeks on one sentence, submitting to journals and stuff. Comedy is fast.

I have a private group on Facebook with nineteen comedians, and we get to say whatever we want because it stays in this group. I posted, "I think I'm going to try for one hundred rejections in the next year." My friend was like, "Oh, let's all do it!" We do a lot of group projects, like, "We're going to do this many shows." I said, "No. This is a me project." They could do it separately if they wanted, but I didn't want other people involved in my plan. I made a spreadsheet and started keeping track.

It was easy to collect rejections, and after the first twenty-five, I started gaining momentum. I posted on my social networks, "I'm aiming for one hundred rejections this year," and people were like, "Holy shit. What a great idea. Keep going!" I felt motivated from their feedback and it just took off from there. I applied for so many things, including comedy festivals or shows for which I felt qualified but didn't have connections. I also applied to things I thought I wasn't qualified for. For example, I'd always been afraid to submit to *The New Yorker*. In my twenties, I was like, "I'm too young to write for 'Shouts & Murmurs.'" Then, in my thirties, I was like, "I think I'm too dumb. I don't have the mental chops for *The New Yorker*." And you don't write a two-sentence pitch; you write the whole damn thing and it takes forever because you want it to be perfect, pouring hours into something that will probably be rejected. But I wrote a piece and submitted it and they were like, "Yeah. We'll run this." Then I submitted again, and they were like, "Yeah."

But a lot of the rejections came from me trying to create opportunities for myself. I reached out to shows, asking, "Do you need a writer?" or "Here's my pitch for you!" I write comedy pilots, so the project included sending out some of those. You just slave over this thing and have no idea if anyone's interested. It's disheartening and you feel like you're in a vacuum.

My favorite comedian is Ophira Eisenberg. Years ago, I wrote her an e-mail that I never sent, telling her how much I admire her writing and her stand-up. During my rejection project, I had the opportunity to write a packet for *Ask Me Another,* an NPR show where Eisenberg is the host, and I obviously jumped at it. I was so nervous because I was like, "She's going to read it!" And I got a job as a regular writer for the show! It is absolutely my dream job. Ophira is the best, and it's so fun to write for a woman.

I'm a night owl, but during my rejection project I decided to try writing for twenty minutes every morning, and it turns out that I'm really a morning writer. I'd never been a morning anything.

EMILY WINTER'S TIPS

TIP 1—I've learned through experience that taking a day off to watch TV or go drink myself silly, those things don't work. After a rejection, the only thing that works is to keep my head down and work on other things, write something else that I can feel proud of.

TIP 2—After I got some publicity for my rejection project, a few people e-mailed me, saying, "I just started comedy a week ago, but I was inspired by your rejections. Can

I do your comedy show?" I'm like, "No! I've been working for years and years to make this show great, to bring in the audience. You should pursue rejections by asking for things that are *a little* out of reach—but not *way* out of reach! Don't put the ball in my court." So I think some people need a push to take chances and put themselves out there, and some people need the opposite: to privately work on their craft instead of overconfidently peddling a bad or mediocre product.

TIP 3—Men are told they're fine as they are, and women are told that we're not fine, so we're always striving. It's not good, but I think it hardens us. Being told you need to strive and there will be bumps in the road prepares you better than being told that you're great and everything you do is great.

SAM JAY

There were so many festivals I didn't get into that
bummed me out, so many showcases where I didn't
make it to the next round. Being a comic involves so
much rejection.

To listen to or watch Sam Jay is to fall a little bit in love. *The
Boston Globe* has written about the comedian's "effortless
honesty and confidence." She has swagger and intelligence, and
she's just really funny. Her first appearance on late-night TV was
Jimmy Kimmel Live!; she's also had a half-hour Comedy Central
special, has been on Netflix's *The Comedy Lineup,* and recorded
her own Netflix special in 2020. Her first comedy album was
called *Donna's Daughter.* She also writes for *Saturday Night Live,*
has been nominated for an Emmy for *SNL,* and shows up often
in sketches.

Growing up in Boston, Sam Jay attended a specialized high
school that encouraged individuality. On the podcast *Las Cultur-
istas,* she spoke fondly of her school, saying that teachers challenged her. "We know what you're capable of," they said. The
school also taught her that learning is not a race, that everyone is
different, that everyone works at a different pace. She told me,
"That whole mindset is how I ended up here"—a comedian who
didn't start doing comedy until her late twenties.

Lessons I've Learned

Even if the work you do is in some way personal, you need to compartmentalize the selling of that work so that you don't take its rejection personally.

I always liked comedy and stand-up. Ever since I was a kid, I would watch Bill Cosby's stand-up, I'd watch Eddie Murphy a lot, Dave Chappelle. I liked sitcoms, *Married with Children,* stuff like that. I was a kid who watched way too much television, and always comedy stuff.

I started to be curious about stand-up when I was about twenty. Then one day, I was just like, "It's something I've always wanted to do," and I decided to try it, weird as that may sound. I didn't write anything but went to a couple of open mics around Boston and got up and did some material. But life interfered, and that was it for several years. I moved to Atlanta and didn't do anything comedic again until much later.

The first time I got back up was when I did this show at the Star Bar in Atlanta. I was twenty-seven and it was about to be my birthday. It was also right around New Year's Day. I remember one comic there was like, "Oh, here come all these people trying to fulfill their New Year's resolution to get onstage," and I was like, "Oh man, I'm one of those people, that's corny."

But sometime later that year, I fully committed. I was at my cousin's house, we were having dinner, and I was telling jokes, and everyone was dying laughing. I was like, "I just gotta try this." I gave myself one year to see what happened. I had never seen people in the business who looked like me—it was only much later that I saw the work of Gina Yashere and Nikki Carr, who are masculine-presenting lesbian comics.

I called up my cousin, whose husband had actually been a comic since I was a kid. I asked her husband where to go and he was like, "Oh, I got this show you can come to Sunday." I went and did that show and remember feeling like, "Okay, this is cool," even though I got booed. I didn't get discouraged or take that personally, because people weren't there to see me. Another comic that night told me about the other open mics in the city, and I just started going.

I did a lot of open mics after that, eventually booked gigs. I did comedy festivals and a lot of showcases—they do those in New York, LA, or San Francisco. You do one minute of comedy and get some exposure. The top people from those places go to LA to do one big showcase. It's about getting your face out there in front of the right people so that you can be in the right conversations. Relationships might come out of it, or a late-night booker might be like, "Hey, we'd love for you to do *Kimmel* if you send us a good tape." At one point, I was one of the top comics in Boston, but I went to New York, did a stand-up NBC showcase, and got eliminated the first round. I was like, "Oh, that sucks," but I also remember thinking, *Okay, those motherfuckers are good.* But the second time, I got to the finals; by the third time, I had a manager.

Being in those showcases taught me how to be judged. Initially, I took rejection a bit more personally because the work I'm doing is all so personal. But then you get to a place where you realize it's a business for people. At the end of the day, it's your art but it's other people's business and they're going to treat it like a business. You have to learn how to make those distinctions for yourself and compartmentalize things.

You don't have to take every opportunity; it's okay to reject the ones that don't feel right.

One of the New York showcases was a "diversity showcase," which meant it was for women and queer comics and people of color, and unlike the usual showcases, it was open call. People waited in line outside all night, sleeping outside, and getting in was first come, first served. The networks get so much shit for not being diverse, so they were trying to focus on diversity for this particular showcase. If you won, then you got a development deal with NBC or something. But in a regular showcase, comics don't have to wait on a line. You're either invited or not, so it bugged me that the diversity showcase was crowds of people in the streets. I thought it was kind of shitty to make people wait outside like that.

Because I had a manager, I didn't have to wait outside, but I remember that I got on the stage and was like, "I'm not feeling this. This feels gross." I bombed, but I bombed on purpose—or if not exactly on purpose, then because I realized I didn't like the process. This was not the way I wanted to win. At that point, I was a pretty well-known comic and I think it was like, "Oh, Sam didn't want to be here," you know what I mean? But I just wasn't feeling it.

That was a moment that taught me you don't have to take everything. I want to create enough avenues for myself profes-sionally that I can make the stuff I want to make, but doing this was not the way I wanted my opportunities to come. I realized that I got to decide what kind of artist I was going to be.

I ended up moving to LA and got this Comedy Central Comics to Watch showcase, which is when it all started to come together. The biggest comedy festival, the Just for Laughs Comedy Festival in Montreal, invited me.

I went to JFL in Montreal and was invited to New Faces, a series highlighting up-and-coming comics. Some people from *Saturday Night Live* were there, and they saw my New Faces set and liked me and asked my management if I would be willing to audition. I auditioned two or three times, and then I got a call that was like, "We love you, but we don't know if you'll fit the cast. We still want you to be a part of the show, and we would love it if you came and wrote for the show." I moved back to New York and started writing for *Saturday Night Live*.

That's been a learning process more than anything else. I've grown as a writer, which has been valuable. I can see how plots are set up, can understand how a story should move along; I see holes in a script more quickly. I write with people all the time, because at *Saturday Night Live,* you split off from the group and write with anyone you vibe with. Then you turn it in, they pick sketches, you do a big table read, and they pick the show.

As often as not, your sketch is not chosen, and that can be frustrating. There are times where I thought I wrote something that should be in and it's not, but everybody goes through that. Everybody has written stuff they felt should be in and isn't. It's the nature of the job, so it's kind of like—you're upset and then you've just got to move on.

SAM JAY'S TIPS

TIP 1—There's no one route to becoming a comic. You've just kind of got to do your own thing and trust yourself. And get up a bunch. If you want to be good, you just need to get up onstage and perform a whole lot, dealing with rejection over and over.

TIP 2—Remember that you are also allowed to be the rejecter and say no when something is posed as a great opportunity but just doesn't feel right.

CHELSEA SUNDAY KLINE

After running for office, you realize that the world doesn't collapse even if you lose.

Chelsea Kline's daughter, Lulu, wrote to our local paper when Chelsea was running for state senate. "I would vote for my mom even if she wasn't my mom," she wrote. "Because of her lived experiences as a teen mom raising me, working hard but still needing food stamps and MassHealth, she instinctively understands the urgency with which people need support mentally, financially, and systematically in order to flourish." Kline ran with a promise to support the most vulnerable in our communities. She'd been doing this work for years, but never as an elected politician. "I was in so many feminist spaces," she said, "but those always felt like they were pushing from the outside for inclusivity. It didn't occur to me that it was important for me to insert myself more into the mainstream."

I met with Kline on a Monday morning in my home, a bag of cough drops between us because we were both getting over colds. We had known each other casually for years, but I'd never had the chance to sit and hear what led her to a first political campaign in 2018. When the interview was over, I was ready to join up and work on her next campaign.

Lessons I've Learned

There's no "right kind of person" who's supposed to be in government.

At eighteen, I was living in Virginia and working at a health food store when I accidentally got pregnant. I wasn't sure what to do. I went to the abortion clinic and sat in the waiting room but thought, *Nope. I want to have a baby. I'm going to be a mom.* I'd had a turbulent, wacky childhood, and this felt like it would be grounding for me and would make me grow up. I think because I had a choice, with access to a safe and legal abortion, I was able to really embrace motherhood.

Then having a baby woke me up a little bit politically, because I wanted every woman to have the same autonomy over her body that I'd had. I got involved in reproductive justice, volunteering with the Feminist Majority, with Planned Parenthood—just wherever opportunities came up. I was like, "Here I am, a baby on my hip, and I want to be involved."

I moved to DC and became a nanny, working for three or four families and living pretty close to the bone; for a while, my daughter and I were on food stamps. One of the mothers I nannied for was this amazing woman who had been a counterterrorism agent with the CIA. I loved her and her kids, and she mentored me, asking, "What's next? You're not going to be a nanny forever. You're too smart and the world needs you." She was a big catalyst in my life.

College was next. With my mother and my young daughter,

I moved to Northampton, Massachusetts, enrolling at Smith College as a nontraditional student majoring in religion. During senior year, one of my professors encouraged me to apply to Harvard Divinity School, and I did—and shocked myself by getting in. So many of the skills that I learned at divinity school had to do with being an active listener, a non-anxious presence, and helping people to come to their own conclusions during times of transition. Those skills actually led to a job as a career counselor for adult women at a local university.

During this time, I also got married and had two more children and stayed involved as an activist. When Western Massachusetts created an inaugural Commission on the Status of Women and Girls, I applied and was selected to represent my part of the state.

Being a commissioner meant visiting the state house in Boston and talking to elected officials about upcoming votes on bills that were important to me. For example, I would explain why, as a former teenage mother, I thought comprehensive sex education made a difference. I'd never spent time with legislators and was surprised to see they were regular human beings. One state senator had a child with a disability, and I watched her lead the charge to pass legislation that looked out for people with disabilities in her district and across the state. It was amazing. However, it never occurred to me to run for office, I think partly because I didn't have the "right" background, having had a baby when I was a baby, having been on food stamps. I thought I wasn't the kind of person who was supposed to be governing.

Then something happened. A scandal broke involving a

Massachusetts state senator, Stan Rosenberg, who represented Western Massachusetts. His husband had improperly touched employees and had also used the senator's official e-mail to intimidate and harass employees. Accusations were mounting and it was unclear how much Rosenberg knew, but he wasn't stepping down.

What I heard and saw triggered something inside me. I thought of my own small sons. People who worked in Rosenberg's office were talking to the press about feeling unsafe, and I just felt so strongly that it was wrong. There was an election coming up and I decided to challenge Rosenberg. I imagined I'd be the agitator who opened the door, but then others would also realize he needed to be challenged, and they would run against him.

Being in public office is like being a supercharged activist with money.

I wrote a press release announcing that I was going to run for office and sent it to every news outlet in Western Mass. My announcement ran above the fold in the local papers. A team of volunteers came together. Then I had to go with this team to collect signatures and actually get on the ballot. We went all over the district and I got a variety of reactions, from "Oh my God. I love Stan Rosenberg. I won't even sign your papers" to "It's about time. Good for you! We need more women."

I had been a regular person; now others sought my opinions. It was overwhelming and exciting. I pulled in as many experts as I could on environmental policy, transportation, wind energy, public education—I had an advisor for everything. I had to learn how to give a press interview, to be concise and clear about my vision, and to debate. Organizations began endorsing me, including Planned Parenthood and the American Federation of Teachers. Momentum was building as I canvassed, going from door to door and saying, "Hi, I'm running for state senate. Tell me what's important to you." I really wanted to hear from actual people about what worried them and what they needed.

What I heard is that people felt forgotten. There were so many stories of pain and worry. They said, "I work three jobs and I'm barely surviving" or "I can't send my kid to college." When I talked about having been a young mother, having known food insecurity, and then explained what I stood for, countless people would say, "That's so reassuring. How exciting that a real person is running. I really feel like you'll look out for me and protect Western Mass." I wasn't a lawyer and I'd never been in politics, but I was starting to think maybe people like me, people who had struggled, were in the *best* position to be leaders. We would look out for the most vulnerable.

The more I campaigned and the more I spent time with people who worked on Beacon Hill [where the Massachusetts State House is], the more I was like, "Oh, this is like being a super-charged activist. This is being an activist with an actual mouth-piece, and actual money, and actual power." I was like, "Why didn't I aspire to do this earlier? This is wonderful." Another candidate joined the race to unseat Stan Rosenberg, but now I was *in this* and wanted to win.

So I worked hard. I love food, but I think I ate only Clif Bars and water through that entire summer. I barely saw my kids. It was rough. I announced my candidacy in March 2019 and the primary was September 4. In August, I had a virus but was still out knocking on doors, napping in my car. I would be on fund-raising calls, at events, debates, more events.

Then Election Day came. I was so glad the campaign was over, and I felt optimistic—so much energy had gone into lifting up my campaign, so many people were excited! But I didn't win. My ten-thousand-plus votes showed how hard my team had worked, how far we had reached, but it was like running into a brick wall.

The loss was shocking and painful. I live in a small town, and when I went out, friends who hadn't supported my candidacy for whatever reason seemed to be avoiding me, bowing their heads so that our eyes didn't meet. At first I was confused and embarrassed; then I realized, "I was brave and stood for what I believed in. That made them uncomfortable. There are far worse things."

And many people continued to support me, saying inspiring and helpful things. One friend said, "You've been tempered. You just walked through fire and you're bulletproof now. You can do anything." After the initial disappointment, it began to feel that way. People started approaching and asking me to run for mayor. In my thirties, that would have been unimaginable to me; now I can imagine it.

Right after the election, Jim McGovern, our congressman, said, "Chelsea, you've got to continue to maintain a public presence and a voice." He seemed to be already thinking about my next campaign. Around the same time, the editor of our local newspaper asked me to become a columnist. I have been able to write about the issues that are important to me as I think about what I'm going to do next.

Looking back, running for state senate was a little like when you're a kid, you're scared there's a monster in the closet, and you get up the gumption to open the door. You realize, "There's no monster." That's what it was like losing my first campaign. "So what? It didn't happen. I'm still alive. The boogeyman isn't real."

CHELSEA SUNDAY KLINE'S TIPS

TIP 1—If you are thinking about running for office, then you need to make a conscious choice to just put away any self-doubt, just squash it down in an imaginary box and put it away. Self-doubt is a waste of time and energy.

TIP 2—A lot of people don't win their first campaign. That is okay.

TIP 3—Telling women and people from marginalized groups, "You should run for office," is not actually helpful. I ran by the skin of my teeth, tapping every person I knew for five bucks to keep my headquarters open, but I was also employed and had a life partner and connections. So many pieces were in place. We need more systemic support if we want more women and people from marginalized groups to run for office.

ROZ CHAST

I submit like six or seven cartoons every week to *The New Yorker*. A lot of times they buy one, but a lot of times they don't buy any. And it's still horrible to get rejected.

As a native New Yorker, I think of Roz Chast as "my cartoonist"—many people must have this feeling—and so it was thrilling to have a chance to speak with her over the phone. I had been reading her cartoons in *The New Yorker* for years and had also loved her powerful, funny, unsentimental memoir about her parents as their health deteriorated and they died. The memoir, *Can't We Talk About Something More Pleasant?*, was published in 2014. It won a National Book Critics Circle Award and was nominated for a National Book Award. Chast grew up in Brooklyn but spent a large portion of her working life in Manhattan, and her work captures the unspoken knowledge and neuroses of New Yorkers. Chast told the Rumpus in 2017 that she is inspired by walking around the city and added, "I think when you really love something, you notice the minutiae." Chast's other topics, categorized as such on her website, include "fairy tales," "fear and loathing," and "kids and family." It was eye-opening to hear that most of what she does gets rejected.

Lessons I've Learned

When you are used to being "the artist"—or the most talented person in any domain—then putting yourself in any environment full of other talented people can be destabilizing.

In kindergarten, I did not like to play with the little girls who were playing house. My mother was an assistant principal, and I just didn't understand "house." The two bossiest girls got to be the mommies and we were all the slaves. It would be like, "You iron, you do the dishes, and we get to be the bosses." I also didn't like playing with the boys because they were kind of rough, and I didn't like sports. But there was an easel in the back of the classroom, and I would stand there and make pictures. Sometimes there would be one other kid, sometimes not.

When you're a little kid, if you're a really fast runner, you kind of know it because you're always picked for a team. If you're good at math, you get a sort of inkling of that because math is fun for you and you do well on tests, and you start getting known as "the kid who is good at math." I always liked to draw and always got good feedback for it, and then I drew more and got better at it, and that was sort of my thing. I wasn't good at other things. That was it.

I really wanted to get a drawing published in the well-known kids' magazine *Highlights for Children*. It had a section called "Our Own Page," with drawings by kids. However, I noticed when I was around nine or ten that most of the drawings done by little girls were of horses. My family lived in Brooklyn. I never saw horses. I didn't even like them very much. They just seemed like giant animals with these giant jaws. But I thought, *Okay, if I'm going to get on* "Our Own Page" *I should really learn to draw a horse.*

So one day I sat down and made myself draw horses. I had this sketch pad with cheap paper in multiple colors: orange, purple, green. I filled it up with horses, and I named them. There was Whitey and Prancy and a bunch of others. They had faces and expressions. Then afterward, I looked at them and they made me laugh so hard. They were terrible, but there was also something really funny about them. I still remember just laughing like an insane person; they didn't look like horses, they looked like very weird dogs. But I was trying. I never did get a drawing on "Our Own Page," but I got a poem published there.

Throughout high school, I continued to draw a lot, filling sketchbook after sketchbook. Then I was admitted to Rhode Island School of Design (RISD), and I left Brooklyn to go to college. When you have always been the special art person in your class, and then you go to a school where everyone has always been the special art person, it's pretty destabilizing. That's what RISD was like, almost from the very beginning. I'd go to a class and there'd be an assignment and then I would bring my sad little thing in and everybody else's was so much better. I wasn't even in the middle. I was sort of at the bottom as far as drawing skills went.

Meanwhile, what I really loved was drawing cartoons, but my cartoon work couldn't be categorized as "underground" and it wasn't quite "overground." I worried that I would never make a living as a cartoonist, because my stuff didn't fit in. When I learned that this small group of boys had started a cartoon magazine, I was excited. It was called *Fred*. I had found my people! I put together a bunch of drawings and submitted a portfolio to *Fred*'s editors.

Then I waited.

There was a lawn with a hill in front of RISD's freshman dorm, and I remember sitting down on the grass alone after I heard back from *Fred*. They wouldn't take any of my drawings. I just sat on that hill by myself, weeping, crying like a baby. It was really crushing. It hurt a lot.

Rejection might be more about the rejecters than about you. And you might just have the last laugh.

I didn't know why I had been rejected, but I never resubmitted to *Fred*. When the magazine came out, its cartoons were very underground-looking, kind of like imitation R. Crumb. Whatever I was doing was apparently not what they were looking for. Looking back, I don't think they said, "Oh, she's a girl and we don't want her in the boys' club," but maybe there was something about my work that was unlike their work, and subconsciously they rejected it because it was unfamiliar. Now, of course, it's many years later, and one thing I know is that *none* of the editors of *Fred* have gone on to be successful cartoonists. It would be an understatement to say that this fact gives me pleasure.

But the bad news from *Fred* was not my only rejection at RISD. There were many. Art schools don't like it when you come in with a style. Their job is to break you down and take that away. That is sort of what was happening to me. I had teachers tell me that my work was bad and even critique my personality. One teacher said, "You know what, Roz? I have a feeling you're never going to be happy." Who says that to an eighteen-year-old? I should have just said to this person, "And *your point is?*" Now that I'm no longer a teenager, I understand that the teachers are young people themselves, with their own problems. But when you're eighteen years old, you don't know that. You're looking for encouragement and support and guidance.

By the time I got out of RISD, I really felt like I sucked. I felt like, *I hate myself, I hate my drawings, I suck at art. But—I still want to do it.* I think that is something you either know or you don't. To know that you're going to do it, even though you suck . . . it's kind of stupid. It's like you want to run this marathon, even though you have a broken leg and a stoop and you're near-sighted. You're going to run, even if you come in last. Nobody will stop you. You don't even *want* to run, but somehow you have to.

I kept drawing, and once I got to New York, it was like a whole different ball game. I began selling cartoons, first to a magazine called *Christopher Street*—I found an abandoned copy of it on the subway, paged through, and saw that the editors bought cartoons. That was my first paid cartooning job. Then I began selling to *The Village Voice* and *National Lampoon*. But the person who probably changed my life was Lee Lorenz, the art editor of *The New Yorker*. I first submitted my cartoons in 1978. They bought some and continued buying work from me. I'll always be shocked by that, and grateful.

I feel so lucky being able to do what I love to do for a living. The weeks where I don't sell a cartoon, I still think, *They've finally learned how terrible I am and I'll never work again.* All those kinds of things. But at this point, it's just how I think and what I do. After a rejection, I try to forget about it and move on. *The New Yorker*'s weekly deadline keeps me drawing no matter what. And if my work is rejected, I always feel like I have another chance the next week.

ROZ CHAST'S TIPS

TIP 1—Teachers can say asinine things. We want to think we'll get support and encouragement from our teachers, but that's not always the case.

TIP 2—If you not only love to do something, but *need* to do it, then you don't need any advice from me; you're just going to kind of keep doing it, whether or not you're successful. If you stop doing it because you get discouraged, well, maybe actually there are other things you'll love more.

KATE MANNE

Doing anything bold and daring, you're going to ac-
cumulate lots of rejections in the process. That's why
developing a healthy relationship with rejection is
something I really believe in.

One thing about philosophy, Kate Manne told me, is that it
trains you to accept the possibility of being wrong. Phi-
losophers question one another, trying to find holes in one another's arguments—and there's a good chance that *you're* the
philosopher who's wrong. Manne said, "Accepting that is both
scary and empowering, because it's not seen as a disaster to be
wrong. You just have to be wrong in an interesting, thoughtful
way."

Kate Manne is an associate professor of philosophy at Cornell
University, where she has taught since 2013. She grew up in Melbourne, Australia, a straight-A student who avoided rejection at
all costs. At the University of Melbourne, she studied philosophy
(mostly logic), along with computer science. She went to MIT for
graduate school, was a junior fellow in the Harvard Society of
Fellows, and secured a position at Cornell's Sage School of Philosophy. Soon after her first year of teaching there, an episode of
violence at another university spurred her to try to write an op-ed.
The op-ed kept getting longer and eventually became her first

book, *Down Girl: The Logic of Misogyny.* The book received more attention than Manne expected, and during our conversation, she admitted that she hates "talking and thinking about misogyny all the time." However, she believes it needs to happen, and the response to the book makes it clear that Kate Manne's ideas resonate with many people. *Down Girl* was written up in *The New Yorker, The Washington Post,* Vox, *Guernica* magazine, Jezebel, *The Times Literary Supplement,* the *London Review of Books,* and *The Nation,* among other publications.

Lessons I've Learned

If you always protect yourself from rejection, you may not build the emotional stamina you will need to deal with rejection when it happens.

I was a graduate student studying logic in MIT's philosophy department when my advisor, Sally Haslanger, said something that permanently affected the trajectory of my work. A group of us were sitting in the lounge, and Sally came in and we all began chatting. We got on the subject of men and women in our field, and she remarked that some women in philosophy were disproportionately attracted to logic and also to studying the history of philosophy. When you focus on logic, you work on developing a proof; when you study history, you use the original texts. You rarely have to cope with the possibility of being flat-out wrong in a very public way. I think Sally was saying that women gravitate to logic and to the history of philosophy because we are socialized to be cautious, afraid of the potential humiliation of failure. We are socialized to fear rejection from our peers.

That conversation made me want to take more risks, and I began to explore the area of ethics. You can make missteps in ethics in embarrassing and revealing ways, just by making arguments that fail to take into account the ways in which certain lives are quite different from your own. Over time, I got more comfortable with the possibility of being wrong. However, I did manage—for many years—to avoid rejection in my academic career.

As a student, I was always hypervigilant, unhealthily obsessed with grades. I got into my top choices for college and graduate school; I secured a tenure-track faculty position after graduate school. But after getting that first job, I started submitting articles for publication. When you are a professor, obviously you have to publish academic articles to keep your job and get promoted. Right away, I had a dozen rejections in a row.

Having very little experience with rejection, I didn't know how to cope. I remember one time, I was in my therapist's office, talking about how I thought if my work was good enough, if *I* were good enough, then I wouldn't be dealing with rejection. I walked out of his office, checked my e-mail, and saw a message from an academic journal to which I had recently submitted. I clicked on it, and there was yet *another* rejection, this time with several very critical comments that felt devastating to me.

I continued to talk about these rejections in therapy, and I would also go home and talk with my husband. He is an academic too, so we could commiserate. I didn't talk about the rejections with anyone else that I recall. I felt a lot of shame and so I kept them largely private. Inside, I felt like an impostor. It was probably the bleakest professional time of my life.

As I struggled to keep going in philosophy, I dealt with the rejections by trying to respond to every single critique and suggestion that I had received from these journals. I would sit down and rewrite every article, multiple times. The problem with that approach was that while *sometimes* the comments were constructive, with the potential to make my work stronger, other feedback was, "I don't like this article." Then the reader would go into a bunch of reasons why, without offering a single idea about how to improve the content or style. Because you can't please everyone, my habit of rewriting to address everything started to feel like an unhealthily hyperbolic response to rejection.

It's okay to do the work that is most exciting and gratifying, even when those in your field don't think it's the most prestigious.

Over time, I gradually began to figure out which criticisms were worth responding to, and I revised my articles well enough that they began to be accepted for publication. Recently, I received tenure, which was a huge relief and life milestone. But fairly early on during my tenure-track job, I realized that publishing in academic journals, even the most prestigious ones, was not necessarily my highest priority. Part of that was due to the topics I became most interested in and the venues that seemed more suitable for their discussion having a broader reach and a somewhat more general audience.

In May 2014, I had just finished my first year of teaching when I learned that a twenty-two-year-old man named Elliot Rodger had killed two women near a sorority house at the University of California, Santa Barbara. Rodger had dropped out of a local community college and had been posting YouTube videos along with a so-called manifesto about his plan to seek retribution against the "hot sluts" who had rejected him. In reality, he had been stalking the women at the sorority house but in fact had never met them.

Reading the story and listening to media responses, I was struck by the rhetoric around it. It was clearly a gendered hate crime, but many people denied that, despite Rodger's narrative— his sense of toxic male entitlement to the sexual and emotional services of these women. It was as if the real crime was that he'd been deprived of love and sex and attention and affection. I thought of my students, especially all the young women in classes I had taught all year; I thought of the dismal statistics about sexual assault against women on campus. I began to understand Rodger's sense of entitlement as emblematic of a larger systemic problem, and I felt a responsibility to address it in my writing. I sat down and planned to write a thousand-word op-ed but found that I couldn't stop writing. My article eventually turned into an academic/trade crossover book, *Down Girl: The Logic of Misogyny,* which was published late in 2017.

Even though I spent my early career working hard to publish articles in prestigious academic journals, that's no longer where my heart is. Since writing *Down Girl,* I have realized that writing philosophy for a broader audience—what some call "public philosophy"—is the most exciting thing to me personally, at least for the moment. I love to read clear analyses that help me crystallize hunches I've had about social problems or phenomena. I love the feeling that I've understood something in a new way, thanks to an author I've been reading. If I can contribute to that process in my own writing, that's really all I can hope for.

Of course, I continue to teach, and my graduate students are always submitting articles to journals; they have to in order to build academic careers, and I encourage them to view rejection as an inevitable part of that process. Sometimes a rejection reveals something about your work that can be improved, but often it's fairly arbitrary. I tell them it's important to sustain a sense of your own projects and your own merits, not to have any shame about being rejected. Even while they realize that prestigious journals have a ninety-five percent rejection rate, getting rejected can still feel awful, of course. I tell them to see rejection as a sign that they are putting their work out there—and that is a good thing.

KATE MANNE'S TIPS

TIP 1—Know that doing your best work may mean you're more likely to get rejected, because you may be going out on a limb.

TIP 2—I like the advice to "decide on the number of rejections you need to rack up" (I forget where I originally heard this). I encourage my students to plan on racking up fifty rejections in order to find the sympathetic reviewer who comments, "This is an original, interesting project," and who accepts the piece, or at least helps you to improve it.

TIP 3—At the same time that you send off a piece of writing to a journal, address a separate e-mail submitting it to a different journal. If your article gets rejected, don't spend too long looking at the comments. Unless the advice is compellingly helpful, just send it straight back out again.

PART 4

Take a New Path

My mom and my mother-in-law both switched careers in their thirties, and the stories they've told me about work have always made me feel like it's normal to make a change when things don't feel right.

My mother-in-law was a college writing counselor for seventeen years. She was committed to her students and had many friends among the faculty, but the writing center was small and there was always a feeling of being "less than" among the professors with their PhDs. Certain moments reinforced that feeling: For example, every student had to write a thesis in order to graduate, and struggling seniors would bring her hundreds of pages of half-formed thoughts. Their professors were not available to help them organize, synthesize, and create, so at the writing center she'd sit with the students for hours, over many weeks, until they had papers that made them proud. Then when graduation came, these same students would give speeches about how grateful they were for the expert guidance . . . of their professors. It wasn't like my mother-in-law needed to be constantly thanked, but a little something would have gone a long way. And it was part of a pattern.

Over the years, she talked with so many students about their writing anxiety that she decided to return to school for psychology. She was intellectually curious but also wanted the status she felt she'd have with a doctorate. This led to a complete career change. My mother-in-law became a psychologist, got a job at a university counseling center, and had a successful twenty-seven-year career. She's now retired from the university but still sees patients as part of a psychotherapy practice.

My mother *also* switched careers in her thirties, leaving her job as an English teacher and going back to school for . . . *wait for it* . . . psychology.

After earning her doctorate, she was hired as a school psychologist, and the outgoing person in the job offered some advice: "Don't make the same mistakes I did! Ask for more support in order to do your work!" She advised my mom, for example, to request an office that was not in the school's basement.

Looking back, my mom says, "I assumed she knew what she was talking about, but she didn't—and I shouldn't have listened." As soon as my mom broached these requests with the school's principal, the principal said, "Forget it. Don't come." My mom was fired before even starting the job.

It was devastating. She had been counting on the school position for our family's healthcare. My dad had just left *his* job, and there was no money coming in. My mom called a supervisor who knew her and said, "I need work!" Ultimately, she secured a part-time job at a different elementary school. My mom had always wanted to be her own boss—that was the whole reason she'd gone back to school—so on days she wasn't there, she started building up a private practice.

Over the years, I've absorbed so many lessons from my mom and my mother-in-law. They're each resilient. They each were able to change course, following entirely new career paths even though they had young kids and faced many unknowns. My mother-in-law gradually began to tell a new story about who she was and what she was capable of. My mom knew from the start that she valued being her own boss; this helped her to persevere even when things got rough.

Some of the women in the upcoming section talk about realizing that they weren't well matched to their jobs—and rejection was just what they needed in order to pivot. Carolina Miranda started a blog that ultimately led to a job at the *Los Angeles Times*. Pamela Shifman was rejected from every clerkship, but this reminded her she actually didn't want to be a law clerk or a lawyer. Unmi Abkin started her own restaurant after she couldn't find work as a chef.

So many demands are made on women that we have little time to stop and think about what's important to us. It sounds crazy, but a rejection can provide that opportunity.

TARA SCHUSTER

I've been called "aggressive"—which is a term that gets thrown at women. The thing that I wish I had known earlier was just not to take it so personally.

Tara Schuster believes in taking action first and asking permission later. When confronted with a new open-plan office, she discreetly set herself up in a small conference room, knowing she needed quiet in order to concentrate. I was struck by her chutzpah—if you're not familiar, it's the Yiddish word for bravery—and asked how she *got* like that. Schuster told me that she had had to be that way while growing up "underparented." She tells the story of her childhood and young adulthood in a memoir, *Buy Yourself the F*cking Lilies: And Other Rituals to Fix Your Life, from Someone Who's Been There,* which starts with her description of a rock-bottom moment long ago when she drunk-dialed her therapist. When we spoke, Schuster had actually just finished the book, having written every morning before going to work, plus a lot of weekends. It was published in 2020, received glowing reviews, and was highlighted by *People* magazine.

Meanwhile, Schuster had a full-time job as vice president of talent and development at Comedy Central. She scouted scripts and comedians, then nurtured and created a lot of amazing content. She was the executive in charge of *Lights Out with*

David Spade and oversaw the development of multiple shows, including *Another Period* and *Hood Adjacent,* and the Emmy and Peabody Award–winning comedy series *Key & Peele,* which is one of the best shows of all time, in my opinion. In 2020, she left Comedy Central to pursue writing and TV development.

Lessons I've Learned

Getting rejected can lead you to take initiative in ways you wouldn't have imagined.

I grew up in Los Angeles and went to college at Brown with plans to become a playwright, but after working in the New York theater scene, I realized playwriting would be a struggle. Writers around me were making beautiful work, but writing plays seemed like a hard way to pay off student loans, of which I had many.

I decided to explore television and applied for an internship at *The Daily Show,* which was a life-altering experience. The rigor of that show, the thoughtfulness in the writers' room, matched the process of the best playwrights. Scripts were so well done and funny and incisive that I decided that I definitely wanted to work in TV. But other than that one internship, I had no TV experience—legit none.

When the *Daily Show* internship ended, I applied for the first Comedy Central job that came my way: digital production assistant at Comedy Central's website Jokes.com. Part of the application asked, "Can you write HTML?" and I was like, "Of course I can." I couldn't at all. I just knew I'd figure it out.

You've seen video clips online? Somebody had to create the files containing those clips, and I was that somebody. It was the absolute last rung on the ladder to Hollywood—not even the ladder, maybe the ditch that you had to climb out of to reach the ladder. The work was meticulous, mundane data entry, but I got to watch every Comedy Central stand-up special ever, so I got an education in both digital media and comedy. At the time, well-meaning adults further in their careers were saying, "Follow what you're passionate about." I wasn't passionate about building video records, but I was learning new skills. Eventually I got a reputation for being smart and responsible, someone who would get things done.

After two years of sitting alone in a cubicle and building these forsaken video records, I was excited to learn about an opening for digital producer on Stephen Colbert's show. It would mean working in the show's offices rather than at the network headquarters. I loved *The Colbert Report* and while the job didn't mean I'd be writing plays, I would be around writers and in a creative environment.

I applied internally at Comedy Central and went confidently through several rounds of interviews. I was well respected and had credibility, so I thought, *I'm going to get this and it's going to be awesome.* I would work with Stephen Colbert and it would change my life.

Then the phone call came. I was in the West Village in front of a ramen restaurant when I picked up the call from Comedy Central's Human Resources division and learned I hadn't gotten

the job. I remember standing on Seventh Avenue and just bursting into tears. *I've done every unglamorous job you possibly can do,*
I thought miserably. *I've proven that I'm responsible and they won't
give me a chance to work on this show.* I thought my career had
dead-ended. I was heartbroken.

Of course, I had to show up for work the next day, and the
next. I kept showing up and doing my best, even though I felt
discouraged. I figured out that they thought I had been too junior
to be offered the position, but that didn't make me feel much
better.

And then one day I was walking down the hall in Comedy
Central's offices and I passed a set of closed doors where a pilot
screening was going on. Comedy Central airs pilots internally
when they're deciding whether to pick them up. I hadn't been
invited but I knew nobody would notice if I snuck in. I cracked
the door and slipped into a seat in the back. They were airing the
pilot for *Key & Peele,* deciding whether or not to pick it up. It was
the most amazing piece of comedy I'd ever seen.

I had to be a part of this show. I came up with a plan. I was
young—I'd connect with their intended audience—and had
been doing digital media, so I'd know how to distribute *Key &
Peele* online. I went to the higher-ups and pitched myself, explaining why they should hire me as digital producer. The job
was mine.

Being called "aggressive" is not the end of the world.

My new job with *Key & Peele* was based on this question: How
do you translate a TV show to the internet, making it digitally

savvy and expanding its footprint? This meant that I needed to watch every sketch and then actually talk with Jordan Peele and Keegan-Michael Key about what clips should go online.

At first, our relationship was purely professional and somewhat distant. But as things progressed, I showed them my passion for their show and my diligence by setting up social accounts, pitching in on anything that needed doing, and proactively pitching stunts we could do on digital. I gave them everything I had to give, and through my actions, Jordan and Keegan saw they could trust me.

When they came up with the idea for a web series in which Keegan and Jordan would play two of their own viewers—two TSA agents offering critiques of the show—I figured out not only how to execute it but also how to make it a fan favorite, something just as good as the TV show.

I ended up producing the web series, which was called *Vandaveon and Mike*. I'd choose a sketch to "critique," then oversee the edit and give it to Jordan and Keegan for approval. *Vandaveon and Mike* ended up being nominated for an Emmy!

Producing, editing, and hand-delivering video drives when we had to hit tight deadlines hadn't been in my job description; it was more like I took on the job, which could have been very small, and did it to the absolute top of my ability. Ultimately, I developed a real friendship with Keegan and then Jordan and moved to LA to work more closely on the show. I transitioned from digital producer to being the executive in charge of it, and my career completely pivoted to development.

If I had gotten the job on Stephen Colbert's show, I would have been so excited, but much less likely to sneak into a pilot screening uninvited. And my whole career sprung from the decision to sneak into that room!

My job at Comedy Central became about finding an idea and then supporting it, trying to get it on television or online. I looked for new comedians but also worked with veteran writers. Once I'd identified an idea or talent, I pitched it to my boss, explaining why I thought it would work. Hopefully, we bought the idea and then it was my job to nurture it—helping with the premise, giving notes on the script, participating in the creation of the pilot.

At work, I have always received lots of positive feedback, but when I do get a piece of negative feedback, I have a habit of taking it personally, like, "This is a rejection of who I am, I feel so misunderstood." I am definitely someone who takes initiative, who is willing to ask for what I need, and I've gotten pushback for it. I've been called "aggressive," which felt demeaning and hurtful. Even though I knew that women are more likely than men to be seen as "aggressive" at work, I had to learn to not take it personally. I also learned to use it as an opportunity to reflect on my own behavior and to look into the soul of the other person. Why were they calling me this? What does that tell me about them? Where are they coming from? What could I learn? What part of me is giving this impression and does the person have any legitimate point?

Eventually I realized that "aggressive" is not the worst thing you can call somebody. It's actually much worse to be called "incompetent" or "bad at your job" or "irresponsible." Those insults would hurt more! I wish I'd known this when I was younger. In general, I think it's so easy to dwell on our mistakes and harder to savor our wins. That's something I'm trying to get better at.

TARA SCHUSTER'S TIPS

TIP 1—I'm trying to get to a place where I'm not on a roller coaster of wins and losses: I'm doing my best; let that be enough.

TIP 2—When something happens at work that feels like a rejection, the first thing I do is to let myself feel it. I pause, honoring my feelings and not resisting. I don't demean them or tell myself that I'm bad, stupid, or wrong for feeling upset about how I feel.

TIP 3—To make myself feel better, I do something that physically honors my feelings and soothes me in the way you would soothe a kid who fell down—the kid scrapes her knee, you kiss the knee. So I treat myself really well: I'll get sushi and watch *Real Housewives,* or I'll get a massage.

ANA HOMAYOUN

I will always remember the day that I got laid off. My mother said, "This isn't the end of the story."

Ana Homayoun worked briefly as an investment-banking analyst before starting her own business—a story that she tells in this chapter. She founded Green Ivy Educational Consulting in 2002, which works with students and consults with schools on how to encourage students to develop executive functioning skills, organization, and time management but also to find a sense of personal purpose. "I have seen so many students change the trajectory of their lives," she told me. She's written for multiple publications, including *The New York Times, The Washington Post,* and *The Atlantic* magazine, and she's the author of three books: *That Crumpled Paper Was Due Last Week, The Myth of the Perfect Girl,* and *Social Media Wellness.*

Ana travels to schools around the world to speak with parents, students, and educators, and she recently started a nonprofit program to bring Green Ivy's work to public schools. Luminaria Learning Solutions and the Life Navigator Middle School Program help middle school students develop skills for social and economic mobility and social, emotional, and mental wellness. She lives in San Francisco.

Lessons I've Learned

Pay attention to the work that brings you satisfaction—and the work that doesn't.

When I was a sophomore in high school, the director of guidance and counseling took me aside one day and said, "There's this kid who's failing chemistry and I know you're getting an A. He's a senior, and if he doesn't pass, he can't graduate. Would you mind helping him?" I agreed to meet with him and I remember that he showed up to our first meeting with an accordion folder stuffed with papers and no backpack. I was shocked.

Over the next six weeks, we went through every piece of paper in that accordion folder and reorganized it. We found triplicate copies of overdue assignments and went through old assignments and new concepts. I realized his disorganization was the root cause of his academic troubles. He passed the class, graduated, and wrote me a thank-you note saying he couldn't have done it without me.

It felt good to see his newfound confidence and success, and I kept working with and helping other students.

At the same time, I always felt a bit out of place socially. My parents immigrated to the United States from Iran in the mid-1970s, and in middle school my family moved from rural New England to the heart of the Silicon Valley. I attended a private Catholic high school and wasn't familiar with many of the norms my classmates and their parents took for granted. As the eldest child, it was up to me to figure things out and convince my parents to let me participate. Simple things like going to a school dance required weeks-long negotiation. Teachers and counselors were helpful, but most couldn't appreciate how exhausting it was to navigate a world where you never felt any sense of belonging. Meanwhile, I was always silently observing, taking notes, and researching details that were unfamiliar to stay two steps ahead.

I went to college at Duke, in 1999, and while I was there I figured out investment-banking positions were coveted by my peers. I knew nothing about the kind of work investment bankers actually did—my parents didn't work in finance—but I learned the work apparently paid well and had prestige. That next year, I sent a well-crafted e-mail with my résumé to a Duke alumna I found in the alumni database; she helped me get an internship at a top investment bank in the summer of 2000.

When I arrived for summer analyst training, I quickly realized that most of the other interns were extremely well connected. For example, my cubicle was next to a guy my age whose previous work experience was as a lifeguard at his family's country club. On our first day in the office, the head of our investment-banking division walked in, slapped him on the back, and boasted, "Hey, just had lunch with your dad!"

I had spent every previous summer since I was fourteen working at different retail and food-service jobs, and those experiences helped me figure out how to navigate this new world. Even though most of the tasks were mundane, I could manage them and stay organized, communicating effectively with adults. I learned "the uniform," spending my housing allowance—money given to summer analysts to assist with housing, which I pocketed since I lived at home—on silk sweater sets from Banana Republic, appropriate-length skirts, slacks, and flats. At the end of the summer, I ended up securing one of the top reviews and received a full-time job offer for after graduation.

On the whole, I didn't enjoy the work. I did, however, feel a sense of great pride that I received a full-time job offer. This was in the fall of 2000, just as the economy was starting to crumble. My parents thought I should take the offer, and I did. After my graduation, I flew to New York City in the summer of 2001 to attend a ten-week investment-banking analyst training. Although I had made a few friends, it was mostly a lonely summer spent in an extended-stay hotel near Penn Station. Each weekday morning, I'd take the subway into the World Trade Center station, feeling miserable. On weekends, I would wake up super-early and spend hours walking around Manhattan. Of course, I couldn't have imagined how close my subway station would be to the disaster of 9/11—planes would strike the Twin Towers not two weeks after my training ended.

Meanwhile, a personal near disaster threatened my life. One Friday in mid-August 2001, I came home from work with a bad stomachache, initially thinking I had food poisoning. By one A.M., I had called my parents in California. By three A.M., I was borrowing cash from the front-desk clerk at my hotel to take a taxi to the emergency room at St. Vincent's Hospital.

I sat in the waiting room by myself for hours, as everyone else seemed to have some sort of bloody injury. I begged and cried and eventually they took me in for a scan. The doctor said, "You'll need your appendix out right now," and I was rolled into the operating room for emergency surgery. He told me later that I'd nearly died.

But I was okay. My mom flew out to meet me at the hospital and stayed for a few days as I began to recover. As soon as I was cleared to fly, I returned to the West Coast, where I was supposed to begin work in the bank's Palo Alto, California, office. I was too scared to take several weeks off like my doctor recommended and was back at my desk within ten days.

My second day of work in Palo Alto was 9/11. I was safely in California, but my friends in New York were walking to work and taking the subway that horrific morning. For months afterward, I kept replaying memories from the summer and seeing photos of the destroyed spaces I had once walked through every day. It was frightening to think about how close I had been to the World Trade Center throughout the summer.

And now there was a newly unnerving element to my daily experience: Disparaging and racist comments were being made openly in our office, partly because I am pretty sure most of my co-workers didn't realize I was Middle Eastern. I don't look white, but people usually aren't certain what to make of my ethnically ambiguous looks. I went out of my way to keep my personal and professional lives separate, though two of my new supervisors who definitely did know about my heritage went out of their way to make my life difficult. As a recent college grad in a post-9/11 world, I didn't have the courage to complain and was pretty certain anything I said would be ignored or would make things worse. At the time, I was just happy to have a job.

To this day, I think those supervisors taught me "how not to be a boss." It was typical to receive voice mails at eight o'clock on a Saturday night, asking for a nonurgent project to be done by

Sunday morning. They created busywork and a culture of fear that left me on edge. Even when I did everything right, it was inevitably wrong.

In November 2001, I was laid off. The company had initially offered buyouts, and I considered it, but I was afraid to give up a job when the job market seemed dire. Then the decision was made for me.

I remember initially crying after I was let go but then feeling an overwhelming sense of relief. Between 9/11 and my emergency appendectomy, I realized I didn't want to die creating Excel spreadsheets and perfecting PowerPoint presentations in a windowless cubicle. I didn't want to spend my limited time and energy navigating nonsensical office politics. Even though I watched a few well-connected, less-capable colleagues keep their jobs, I didn't feel jealousy or regret. What initially felt like rejection was actually a redirection. I realized I was being purposefully sent—or shoved—in another direction.

In a moment of transition, take time to think about everything you've done workwise, even some of the work that never felt like part of a "career."

Over the next few days and weeks, I asked myself what felt most important and meaningful—and discovered I already knew. I loved the work I'd done in high school. I loved working with teens.

Soon after, I drove to my high school to find that same guidance counselor who had long ago asked me to tutor. "I just want to work with kids again," I said. I had gotten a severance package from the bank and could afford to take some time doing work that felt good. I thought I'd tutor just until the next thing came along.

I began to experiment with the organizational system I'd developed years earlier to help my classmate in chemistry. I started formalizing that system, first meeting with students at their homes. We went through backpacks and binders and filed loose-leaf papers, and I demonstrated how to use planners, manage distractions, and turn in homework on time. As students' confidence soared, so did mine. Within four months, my schedule was full. When the investment bank called six months later to see if I would be interested in coming back as an analyst, I declined. When a friend called to tell me about another opening in finance, I passed on the referral to a friend who ended up getting the job. In two years, I had my own office, went back to school to get a master's in counseling, and happily continued my work.

Now, nearly two decades later, I run a small business working with students and consulting with schools on how to encourage students to develop executive functioning skills, organization, and time management, and to find a sense of personal purpose. The focus of my work has shifted over the years—first with increased technology in schools, and then with remote learning. Still, all these years later, I continue to love the work I do.

I believe that when you're a person of color, especially a woman of color, you become vulnerable when you base your sense of approval on the outside world—on a job title at a fancy firm, for example—instead of designing your own blueprint. My life's work is about helping kids—and adults—create their own blueprints for success rather than borrowing someone else's.

ANA HOMAYOUN'S TIPS

TIP 1—For much of my childhood and young adulthood, I was never allowed to think about how other people's biases or prejudices could contribute to rejection. I now recognize that because bias and discrimination are real, denying their existence can be incredibly harmful.

TIP 2—Part of dealing with rejection as a woman of color is realizing that even if you work twice as hard and are super-prepared, some people will just not like you or will question you or will find reasons to actively reject you. That's exhausting. At the same time, it can be easier to navigate rejection when you feel like you are doing purposeful work, your life's work. That awareness provides a sense of meaning and perspective that insulates you from others' opinions or tangential rejections. It is also critically important to cultivate a network of supporters and clarifiers to provide personal and professional guidance.

JESSICA BENNETT

I have a tendency to dwell on rejection, but if I let it derail me and interfere with my writing, even for a week, then I've lost a week of productivity (and when I was freelancing, income). So I try to maintain perspective. Everyone is constantly telling me to exercise or do yoga—which I'm sure are extremely useful things for a person to do—but instead I go to therapy and I walk my dog, which would have been a useful thing to discover a few years ago when I was freelancing and often didn't leave the house for days at a time. Even if just for the forty-five minutes I'm walking him in the morning, it forces me to get outside of my head.

Growing up in Seattle, Jessica Bennett didn't call herself a feminist. She studied journalism in college, not women's studies. When she began working at *Newsweek* during her twenties, she saw her male colleagues—journalists just starting out, those she'd come up with—being disproportionately promoted. "I was like, huh, something about this feels unfair . . ." She started talking to female colleagues at the magazine, who had noticed the same thing. "All of us had grown up in that kind of 'girl power' era of the eighties, when we were taught that we could accomplish anything, that our gender wouldn't hold us back," she told me. They realized that wasn't necessarily the case. Bennett and two female colleagues began covertly investigating the history of gender bias at *Newsweek* and uncovered a culture of exclusion dating back to the 1970s. In 2010, the magazine published their story, "Are We There Yet?," which looked at what had—and hadn't—changed for women at *Newsweek* and in media more broadly. Bennett says that researching and writing that piece was a wake-up call. It was the start of her career as a journalist who reports on current topics through a gender lens.

In 2016, Bennett published the bestseller *Feminist Fight Club,* which has been translated into twelve languages, expanded into a podcast, and is being adapted for television. The following year, she became the first gender editor of *The New York Times.* Her second book, *This Is 18,* came out in 2019 and was based on her work at the *Times* documenting the lives of eighteen-year-old young women all over the world.

Lessons I've Learned

Small rejections that come with the territory of journalism helped me to build the emotional stamina for managing a big rejection.

The life of a journalist in the modern age is one series of rejections. As a freelancer, your whole job is to pitch and pitch, because half of your ideas are rejected. The publications themselves can also be unstable. My first-ever internship was at my hometown paper, the *Seattle Post-Intelligencer,* now defunct. I moved to New York and worked for an investigative reporter at *The Village*

Voice, which was sold to another media company while I was there. During the time I was at *Newsweek* as a staff writer, the magazine was sold by the Washington Post Company, put up for sale for one dollar, and bought by a wealthy stereo magnate who passed away shortly after, leading to a merger with the Daily Beast. That lasted for a couple of years, but I got out before the divorce, leaving to run editorial for what seemed at the time to be a more stable—and much cooler!—option, a tech company called Tumblr.

Tumblr (before it was bought by Yahoo!, before it became a porn receptacle, back when it was seen as the cool new storytelling platform) was in Manhattan's Flatiron District, which at the time was called Silicon Alley because there were a bunch of tech companies there. I was well paid and there were nice snack options, but the company was still relatively small. Our office was above a strip club, and it wasn't particularly fancy.

Tumblr was trying to make the platform more serious by hiring established journalists to tell the stories of their community. Basically, our job was to come up with creative ways of covering politics and culture. We made some beautiful stuff, like a visual documentary about the so-called *New York Times* morgue, which exists in a sub-sub-basement of the building next door to the *Times* and holds more than a century of old archives and photography. (The *Times* was using Tumblr to showcase that old photography.) We covered the 2012 presidential debates through live GIF making, which was the first time anyone had done that. We partnered with outlets like *Mother Jones* and WNYC to cover the massacre at Sandy Hook and Hurricane Sandy.

About a year after I started, I was in Los Angeles for work, staying with a friend from high school, when I got a request to join a conference call with my boss, my colleague, and an HR rep. That should have been the first sign. I joined the call, and the HR rep basically told us that there was no need for Tumblr to do "journalism" anymore and our team was being let go.

We were pretty stunned. And pissed. The HR person had started like two weeks prior. The company was still a start-up, so there was no real process for anything. We had a million questions about severance and our stock options that they couldn't answer.

The thing is, I always knew I was entering an industry that probably would be unstable; almost every journalist I know has been laid off at some point. This was helpful in that the layoff didn't feel like such a blow to my self-esteem. What was funny was that I thought I was leaving the insecurity of old print media when I went to Tumblr. I had been wrong.

I remember hanging up the phone as my friend Lizzy walked into the room.

I said, "So—I just got fired."

Lizzy was like, "Wait, *what*?" She told me I could stay with her as long as I needed.

We ordered a sushi dinner that night on my company card, which had not yet been shut off. Then I changed my flight to return to New York earlier and upgraded my seat.

Flying home, I thought about what to do next. I had some savings. I planned to file for unemployment, which I did immediately. I was lucky in that I knew I would be fine for at least a couple of months—but what did this mean for my financial future and long-term career? Those were question marks.

A mindset of "I've got nothing to lose!" can be useful if it helps you to imagine new opportunities and be brave.

The next week, I went into the office to clean out my stuff. Sitting at my desk, I thought of a freelance piece I had written for *The New York Times.* It was about women's negotiation training on college campuses, and I had interviewed Sheryl Sandberg, author of *Lean In,* for it. I'd heard Sandberg was launching a digital platform and a nonprofit along with her book, focused on women and work. I knew a little about women and work. I decided to pitch myself for a job.

As a journalist, you constantly have to pitch story ideas to your editor, and often you hear "no." As a freelancer, you're often cold pitching, which means finding the names of editors, guessing their contact information, and introducing yourself along with your story idea. Sometimes you get a response; sometimes you get none. But the primary job of a journalist is to call up people you've never spoken to before and get them to talk to you. Sometimes it's nerve-wracking, sometimes it's uncomfortable, but you get used to people saying no, hanging up the phone, or getting past the awkward small talk to ask the questions you want answered.

So I wrote Sheryl a little pitch about why I thought she should hire me to develop editorial content for her start-up. I was nervous, but I thought to myself, *What's the worst that can happen?* I had no job and nothing to lose. The worst she could do was say no.

She replied immediately and looped in her assistant to schedule a call. Two weeks later, I was flying to California to meet her in person.

Sandberg hired me as a New York–based contributing editor. My job was to think about creative ways for *Lean In* to partner with media organizations to highlight the barriers that still face working women. So, for example, we produced a quarterly section of *Cosmopolitan* magazine called "Cosmo Careers" with stories about women in tech and stay-at-home dads, among other topics.

With Getty Images, we created a photo initiative called the Lean In Collection. Our goal was to repopulate stock photography so that when advertisers or corporate websites or news outlets needed images of, say, a boss, they didn't end up with clichés of white men in suits or a woman in stilettos climbing a ladder meant to represent the corporate hierarchy.

I also pitched myself—multiple times—for a position at *The New York Times*. That started in 2015, when I sat in the office of *New York Times* executive editor Dean Baquet, along with his deputy, Susan Chira, to make a case for why I thought the *Times* should devote a full-time staffer to report on gender (ahem: me). I'd just written a freelance profile of Monica Lewinsky, which I'd heard that Dean had complimented in the all-staff morning news meeting. I knew I had a window of opportunity—so I e-mailed him and asked if he'd be willing to meet. I prepped for days before the meeting and had my talking points memorized. The meeting went great, and Dean and Susan asked me to essentially put my ideas in writing in the form of a memo. I think my memo was ten pages; I thought I hit it out of the park.

But I never heard back from them. Eventually, I ran into Susan in the elevator at the *Times,* and she explained that they had read my memo but the timing wasn't right; there simply wasn't the funding or head count to bring somebody in that position on. We stayed in touch but I basically moved on.

Fast-forward a year and a half, to the fall of 2016. My first book was about to come out and I got an e-mail from Susan telling me that, finally, the *Times* had created a position for a journalist to focus on gender—but as an editor, not a writer. Would I like to apply and write another memo? I just couldn't get it together to do that, not while planning my own book tour, publicity, trying to get the word out.

So I went on my book tour and figured I would try to write for whomever that new gender editor ended up being. But then the election happened. Like many women—and many journalists who had predicted it would be Hillary Clinton—I was stunned by the results. I was equally stunned that a man who had bragged openly about grabbing women "by the pussy" could, and would, be leading our country. What did the election tell us about how America does, or doesn't, value women?

I figured it was a long shot, but I built a website with a new memo. I e-mailed Susan and asked if she would still consider my application.

I got the job.

I think all the little rejections that are part of my life as a journalist helped me to prepare for when there was a bigger one. And I'm still always building my rejection muscles, getting stronger.

JESSICA BENNETT'S TIPS

TIP 1—Try to maintain perspective. My friend Rachel Simmons, who develops leadership programs at Smith College and for women and girls around the world, tells me that she asks her students, "What is the worst that can happen, and can you live with that?" I've tried to employ that sense of "Okay, this is shitty, but my life's not ending. My self-esteem may be hurt, but everyone gets rejected at some point."

TIP 2—Find a confidante. With one of my close journalist friends, I have an ongoing text chain through which we tell each other about our highs and lows as freelancers. One minute, someone has okayed a story idea and you're elated—you feel so competent—and the next minute you get a rejection, and it's easy to think that you suck and are never going to be able to write again. We share all those details and remind each other that rejection is not the end of the world.

CAROLINA A. MIRANDA

I think if this job teaches you anything, it's persistence. You can't be turned off by having somebody refuse to talk to you or to return your call. And that goes beyond talking to sources. It goes to pitching stories and having those stories rejected, or having an editor say, "It might be for us, but you'd have to reformulate it." Or just being ghosted. You have to think: *What are the creative ways of making this story happen?*

When she was a reporter for her undergraduate newspaper at Smith College, Carolina Miranda argued with the editor (another student) about some edits to her news story. The editor got frustrated and said, "If you can't be edited, you'll never make it as a journalist."

Miranda laughed about that story as she told me about the path that led her to the *Los Angeles Times,* where she is a staff reporter. Her articles often explore issues of gender and race as she covers architecture, design, visual art, and film, but—as she phrased it—"I'm also interested in some backyard installation that some dude makes." She seeks out stories that capture the everyday and the absurd, following her interest in what people do aesthetically. "It doesn't have to have a degree or some fancy certification attached to it," she told me.

Prior to her work at the *LA Times,* Carolina Miranda was a

freelance writer and editor, contributing stories on travel and culture to *Time, ARTnews,* Budget Travel, *Travel + Leisure, Lonely Planet, Fast Company,* and WNYC, New York's public radio station. She was also a staff reporter at *Time,* where she worked as part of a team that broke the story of irregularities in FEMA director Michael Brown's résumé in the wake of Hurricane Katrina.

Carolina is a regular guest on *Press Play* on the radio station KCRW and won the 2017 Rabkin Prize in visual arts journalism. She has appeared as a commentator on CNN and on a variety of broadcast programs, including *Good Morning America.*

Lessons I've Learned

When I was growing up, my father worked in heavy construction and we moved around a lot. In the late 1970s and early 1980s, we lived in South Africa and had no phone, no television. Even radio service was limited; half the time we couldn't understand it anyway because it was in Afrikaans and not English. We had to make our own entertainment. My father was working at a cooling plant, which was illuminated at night, so one of our Friday night activities was to get into his pickup truck and drive around the cooling plant. It had all these cool lights and was in the middle of an open grassy plain—it was just this dramatic sight.

As a journalist, I'm interested in reframing everyday things that we may look at regularly but not *see,* and I think my childhood probably helped shape that interest. When the stampede goes in one direction, I go off in another.

I always knew that I wanted to be a journalist but had only a vague sense of what it would entail. No one in my family did that kind of work, and I had no connections. I wrote for my college paper and worked as a desk assistant over the summer at the *LA Times*. As college came to an end, I decided that the thing to do would be a journalism program for new graduates. The *LA Times* has a training program called Metpro for journalists from under-represented communities. I thought, *If I can get into any program, it'll be this one. I'm from LA and I'm Latina.* The program rotated trainees through each section of the paper, through the police beat, reporting on business, then on politics. I imagined I'd follow a traditional journalism path, doing political reporting, then covering the White House or becoming a foreign correspondent.

But the Metpro program rejected me. It stung. I felt like I had potential, and they *knew* me because I'd worked there for a summer. The reality I had to accept was that there were people who were more qualified. And because I was rejected, I started my journalism career down a different path, one that helped me to find the kinds of stories that fit my character, the stories I could best tell. There are writers who graduate from college fully formed; I was not one of those. I was still figuring things out.

When I graduated from college, I worked as a summer intern at *The Nation,* where I fact-checked other writers' stories but didn't do any writing of my own. After that, through sheer grace, I ended up getting a job at *New York Newsday,* as a research assistant for Sydney Schanberg, a columnist there—previously he'd won a Pulitzer as a foreign correspondent at *The New York Times.* That was a really important job for me because he taught me a lot about reporting. I did research; I met with sources; I interviewed government representatives; I wrote up freedom-of-information requests. If Sydney didn't think something was good enough, he would kick it right back to me and I'd have to go back and call sources again. He was very thorough, and he taught me to be thorough too. I also did some writing on the side while I was there, mainly about cultural topics.

Unfortunately, I ended up getting laid off from that job. Out of expediency, I went and worked in public affairs for the New York City comptroller's office; then I took a position in marketing at *People en Español,* followed by a marketing job at *Time* magazine. Those jobs were fun and I used them to learn how the business of journalism worked. But I really wanted to get back to writing. After a brief period freelancing, I managed to get a job as a general assignment reporter at *Time* magazine and covered everything—I might be interviewing Scarlett Johansson one week and rounding up al-Qaeda cases the next. But *Time* was not an ideal fit for me. It was a national magazine, so they were always asking, "Is this a story of national importance? Will a reader in Iowa care about this as much as a reader in Florida?" I was interested in quirkier stuff and in culture, so it was hard to land stories there.

For example, I tried to pitch a story about the freegan movement. This was a network of anti-capitalists in the early 2000s who lived in a way that didn't require consuming—an unusual mindset at the time. Here were highly educated people and artists living in squats and rifling through supermarket trash for food, getting furniture off the street. I hung out with some of them in Manhattan and spent a night going through garbage outside of a supermarket. (I learned that supermarkets have to throw away food at the expiration date, but it's often perfectly good.) Then we all went to somebody's house and cooked what we had retrieved. I did the research and pitched the story to my *Time* editor, but it didn't fly. The editor didn't see enough of a national story to have me reconceive and resubmit it, so that was it.

Part of succeeding at *Time* magazine depended on taking on its strong, institutional voice. It was an important training ground because there were a lot of good writers who could turn out beautiful stories on a dime. But ultimately I knew that if I was ever going to succeed, it would be because my own voice and point of view were recognized. In 2007, they offered some really good buyout packages and I decided to make the leap into freelance. The buyout provided me with a financial cushion to do that.

When I left *Time* it was the 2000s, this beautiful and terrible moment in media. Magazines and newspapers were laying people off left and right. But with the rise of the internet and personal blogs, all of a sudden you didn't need an editor; you didn't have to channel an institutional voice. You could be more informal, cheekier. I started freelancing and blogging, and to my surprise, I managed to attract a small following. The voice I used on the blog began to shape the types of stories I worked on professionally. I think it gave me a more developed eye in finding unusual stories. It also gave me a platform to publish weird stuff if I couldn't sell it.

For example, when I first moved back to LA, there was a doughnut guy in my neighborhood. He would walk around the neighborhood every afternoon, balancing a tray of two hundred doughnuts on his head, and he had this beautiful call that echoed through the hills. In my head, I invented a crazy immigrant tale: He must have been an opera singer in his native Mexico . . . now he had to sell doughnuts! But then I met him and he was like, "Oh no. I sell doughnuts on the side. I'm actually a *luchador*." He was a Mexican wrestler. His whole thing was wrestling, but he could make doughnuts on his own time, be his own boss, and make more money than at a minimum-wage job. It wasn't that the doughnuts were that great, but I thought it was a really interesting story. I sold it to a magazine that was new at the time called *Lucky Peach*. But ultimately it was blogging that made me more alert to those kinds of stories.

Another time, I went to a well-known art fair in Miami Beach and realized visitors were jetting in and out of Miami, having only gone to the art fair at a convention center—so I went exploring. A friend of mine who's Cuban and grew up in Miami took me on a tour of the cemetery where a lot of old Latin American dictators are buried. Her brother had a boat, and we went on a tour around the islands to look at some of the crazy Miami houses. We went to visit the house where Elián González had lived. I did a series of blog posts like, "Hey, if you're in town for the art fair, here are these other weird things that you can see," and other blogs started linking to my stories.

I slowly learned that standing out as a journalist means writing the types of stories that you want to read but aren't seeing. After I'd worked on the blog for a couple of years, a magazine editor at *ARTnews* e-mailed me, saying, "I like your blog. Would you be interested in writing for us?" I almost couldn't believe it: I was being *invited* to write somewhere. I ended up being a contributor at that magazine for many years, which led to other freelance assignments, including for WNYC and *The New York Times* style blog. These, along with my own blog, gave me a public presence and led to my getting hired by the *LA Times*.

At the *LA Times* I'm given a lot of freedom, but sometimes there are still moments when I debate with my editor about what will work and what won't. Sometimes ideas are not fully formed and the editor says, "Go figure it out, then talk to me." Ironically, I now do orientation for the paper's Metpro journalism program—the one I applied to twenty years ago. My first line to young reporters when they're arriving is, "I was rejected from this program, which is a lesson that you should never take no for an answer."

CAROLINA A. MIRANDA'S TIPS

TIP 1—Knowing what you *don't want* is as important as knowing what you want. For an early story at *Time* magazine, I was sent to cover a crime scene. It turns out I'm a terrible crime reporter. But I had to fail at it to learn that.

TIP 2—Sometimes when you're not getting what you want, you're getting something else that's even better, but you don't know that until later. I think at *Time* I was sometimes frustrated that I didn't write more often.

But in looking back, it was this really formative experience in that I ended up assisting writers who were real pros and I got to see how they wrote and learn from that. It was my journalism school.

TIP 3—Journalism is a field that is increasingly difficult to get into. Sometimes I see young people who are quite frustrated by all the nos they are receiving. I think the lesson with journalism is that you just don't take no for an answer. You keep going at it from another angle.

UNMI ABKIN

I couldn't get a job at any restaurants, and I just decided to open my own.

Unmi Abkin was not particularly interested in cooking when
she was growing up in Northern California. She told me
that the closest she got to cooking was "putting cheese together on
a platter" at her parents' bridge parties. She wanted to be a doctor
and graduated from the University of California, Santa Cruz,
with a major in psychology and with all the premed requirements. But at the end of her junior year, she realized she wasn't
ready for grad school yet. She heard about a cooking school in San
Francisco, the California Culinary Academy, and thought it
might be fun. Her parents supported this idea "because I was
kind of sheltered and I think they hoped I'd find a boyfriend."

Today, Abkin is one of the top chefs in the United States. As
of this writing, she has been a semifinalist for a James Beard
Award four years in a row. Her first cookbook, *Curry & Kimchi,*
was co-written with her husband and business partner, Roger
Taylor. The renowned chef Alice Waters of Chez Panisse praised
the book as "joyful and creative" and its recipes as "thoughtfully
balanced, beautifully prepared, and full of vibrant seasonal ingredients." *Curry & Kimchi* was named by NPR as one of the best
books of 2019.

Her restaurant, Coco, in Easthampton, Massachusetts, is my favorite place to celebrate anything or just have a drink with friends because it is cozy and friendly and the food is absolutely delicious.

Lessons I've Learned

Sometimes it's okay to reject an opportunity, even if everyone around you tells you that you're crazy to turn it down.

I had always been a good student, and you could say I was a type A personality, but cooking was the first thing I had ever done where I gave it more than one hundred percent. My cooking school had a bakery that would sell students' food, and I remember learning that my macarons would be sold. I was wearing this tall chef's hat and saw them just out of the oven on one of those rolling racks stacked with trays. I was so excited that I leaned over to gaze at them and burned my forehead.

While in school, I helped open San Francisco's then-new restaurant Boulevard, which is now renowned. They lost a dessert line cook and called me in, asking, "Hey, do you want the job?"

Nancy Oakes, the head chef, really loved me and said I reminded her of herself when she was young. But it turns out I'm not a very good employee. I don't like people telling me what to do. One of my strengths was knowing how to plate food, seeing the plate as a canvas and making it interesting and beautiful. I plated desserts and salads, getting paid about ten dollars an hour.

But after eight months or so, I wanted to move on. The natural progression is that you go from garde-manger to sauté, slowly moving up. It's how you learn. Instead, Nancy opened a new bistro section and invited me to run that.

I'm sure I was impatient; most people would have been grateful: "Wow, Nancy wants me to run the bistro menu." If the chef says she wants you to do that, you just do it. But I was twenty-five, recently out of cooking school, and wanted to keep learning. I gave my notice and made a plan to follow my husband out to the East Coast.

"If you leave now, you're never going to get it back," everyone said—"it" being my success, my rising star, the trajectory I was on. But I was tired of showing people how to plate desserts and put salads together, and I didn't want to run a bistro. I wanted to cook.

My husband was an artist and wanted to live in New York City, but I didn't; Easthampton, Massachusetts, seemed like a good compromise, inexpensive and about three hours away from Manhattan. We got there, rented an apartment, and then I went, "Whoa. Where am I?" There were no cafés in Easthampton, no restaurants (other than diners). No coffee shops.

The only place that would hire me was the Black Sheep in Amherst. I was their baker for about six dollars an hour, glad to have a job, but also a little depressed. I'd gone to culinary school, was super-qualified, and nobody wanted to hire me. Maybe they didn't believe my résumé.

One day I was at my local Northampton video rental place, Pleasant Street Video, complaining that I couldn't get a job cooking, and the nice guy who worked there said, "Hey, I heard about a space downtown that's going to be vacant. You should open a restaurant."

No bank is going to give a twenty-five-year-old a loan, but luckily my family was willing to loan me the money, and that loan allowed me to think creatively. (I later paid it back, with interest.)

The next step to opening a restaurant was coming up with the concept. What was needed? What would fly really well? In San Francisco I'd had an externship at a California-style taqueria, helping create their catering department. I decided to open a place called Cha Cha Cha, a taqueria with some similarities to the place where I had worked, but a lot of differences. I brought in concrete counters and had cement floors dyed cobalt blue. We had corrugated metal and wood stumps from tree trunks in local Greenfield. The restaurant had a super-fresh feeling, like nothing else around—all primary colors and loud music. Almost all the cooks were women when we first started.

I remember the first two weeks we ran out of food every day at eight o'clock, so we'd have to close early. The place quickly became like the community center for Northampton, super-successful.

You may fail once in a while, but that does not mean you are a failure. Learn from your mistakes and then get right back on your path.

But I'm one of those people who can't just coast. I also developed a bit of an ego and thought, *I opened a restaurant at twenty-five and succeeded; I can do anything.* I decided to open my dream restaurant.

There was a space underneath Cha Cha Cha, and I got a huge bank loan to renovate it, writing a business plan that used Cha Cha Cha's income to cover the cost of running this smaller, high-end restaurant. We went over budget on renovation because the underground space had been a bank vault, and I had to blow through thick flooring and walls to put in a staircase. I had a pastry chef, an assistant pastry chef, line cooks, a wood-burning grill. I had ingredients flown in from California, only the best. I was so excited, and so was the staff. I would be cooking my dream menu; there would be nothing like it in Northampton and for miles around. I called the restaurant Unmi.

But within months, it started bleeding money. Not enough people were coming. There just wasn't enough interest in this kind of food, this kind of expense. I could have changed the concept and diluted it, but I thought, *Then why have it?* After nine months, I shut it down.

I was pretty heartbroken. I'd just been hitting my stride with the food. And it might sound strange to say, but when I'd opened Cha Cha Cha, I'd become very popular in town. Everybody wanted to be my friend. Then when my restaurant closed, it seemed like people didn't look at me the same way; it got quiet when I walked in anywhere. I was like, "I'm still the same person!" But there would be this weird, awkward silence. Also, my staff was really upset with me, and some of my closest servers didn't come to help clean up the place after we closed.

Then it was over. I went backpacking for a month with my uncle in the Sierra mountains, to kind of cleanse, and when I came back, I was still just kicking myself: "Why had I let my ego get out of control?" But then I had this idea. Because Cha Cha

Cha ran itself with a competent staff, I asked my two best friends (who had been working with me at Unmi) to drive across the country. We'd spend the winter in Tahoe, where my family had a house, just clear our heads.

As we started that road trip, another local restaurant owner came to me and said, "I hear you might want to sell." Actually, I hadn't been planning to sell Cha Cha Cha, but my marriage to the artist had ended, and I started to wonder if it was time to close the whole chapter.

I sold the business on my drive across the country, and by the time I reached California, it was done. The buyer also bought my condo—the whole package. So what had started as a trip for the winter ended up being a new life.

Luckily I could go home and kind of lick my wounds and figure out what I wanted to do next. I started taking a lot of yoga and thought, *I'll be a yoga instructor!* But it was too touchy-feely. I like to practice yoga, but I don't like to touch sweaty people I don't know, and there's a lot of touching and sweat. Then I decided to study nutrition and worked part-time as a private chef.

A few years went by. I married one of the best friends with whom I'd traveled across the country. Roger and I bought a house, and our daughter was born in 2009. When I thought about my future as a mother, I knew that I wanted Coco to see me as a strong woman, as someone who worked hard doing something she loved. We also didn't want to raise her in California, and Roger's family was in Massachusetts. We decided to move back east.

We wanted to open a restaurant in Northampton but could only find a spot in Easthampton, the place where I'd started out long ago, wondering, *Where am I?*

As we began planning the restaurant, named for our daughter, Coco, everyone said, "Why are you doing that? No one's going to come to Easthampton."

I was like, "They're going to come." And they did.

UNMI ABKIN'S TIPS

TIP 1—Stop listening to the negative voices in your head that make you doubt; they are not real. You have the power to make your hopes and dreams become a reality.

TIP 2—Choosing to be a chef, you need to love it. It's not about money; it's not about fame. When I have students working in my kitchen who seem to be truly talented, I will ask, "Do you want to take this path? Because it's a very, very hard road. You need to really love what you're doing."

MARISSA HABY

Don't give other people (especially supervisors) so
much power—don't rely on outsiders to validate your
worth.

It was my first time on the Google campus, and I was a little
starstruck by the cafeterias, with their free lunch buffets, and
the massage rooms (yes, massage rooms), where employees could
book at a reduced rate. Marissa Haby had invited me to visit
Google on behalf of her supervisor, this very cool guy named
Savio Barretto who had read *Mistakes I Made at Work*, but most
of our communication had been via e-mail. While we waited for
my lunchtime workshop to start, Marissa and I sat down and I
had to know: "How did you end up here?" She proceeded to tell
me the story that follows, which I thought was pretty stunning.
(There is a total creep boss involved.) Later, she took me on a tour
of Google so that I could see the outdoor pool (love) and volley-
ball court and many other special-treatment kinds of things that
Googlers get. Marissa loves her job as global partner marketing
manager in Google's Platforms + Ecosystems Partnerships. She
travels all over the world. When I got back to Massachusetts, I
couldn't stop thinking about the story she'd told me and I asked,
"Would you tell it for the book?"

Lessons I've Learned

I put my heart into everything that I do, and my manager's rejection took a toll on me. I had to learn that my work self wasn't my whole self.

I grew up in a small town called Hillsborough, New Jersey. I loved to dance and thought I would do it for the rest of my life. I attended Rutgers University, a public school in New Jersey, which has a great dance program, the Mason Gross School of the Arts, as well as a renowned business program. I realized I could express myself creatively through both—in dance, we were often telling a story through movement, but there was also storytelling in marketing.

After college, I was recruited by a company near my home, Philips Lighting in Somerset, New Jersey, and soon returned to Rutgers for my MBA, taking classes at night. When one of the more senior members left the company, I was asked to take a leadership position while we looked to hire her replacement. I did that for about six months, and then we hired a new director, to whom I reported.

At first, I would sit in on the leadership meetings with him to help him get up to speed—I'd been on the team a lot longer than he had, and I was used to being part of those meetings, thinking about company strategy and offering input. Once he got more familiar with everything, he continued to ask for my recommendations but told me I was no longer needed at the meetings.

After this manager had been leading the team for a few months, it was time for our biannual performance review. As a company, Philips was generally keen to grow people, to find them new learning opportunities. I put together the "business case" for my value to the company. In addition to my predefined scope, just having been able to keep things afloat before he had been hired was, in my mind, a measure of success.

I sat down with him in one of our glass-walled meeting rooms, took a deep breath, and said, "Here are all the reasons why I feel that I deserve a promotion." He looked at me coldly. He responded that he hadn't gotten his bonus for that year and reminded me that my role was to make him look good. He shrugged his shoulders. It was then I realized I clearly *hadn't* done a good enough job. I wasn't deserving of a promotion.

I felt destroyed. All the hard work, all the extra hours that I'd been putting in while finishing my MBA—how much more of myself could I invest in this job? It had taken so much courage for me to ask, and now I was being turned down.

Instead of being frustrated with my manager, I beat myself up over his rejection. It was like I needed his validation, and not having it meant that I wasn't good enough. My attitude was that at the end of the day, my manager decided who was doing a good job. If he didn't believe that I was succeeding, then why should I? I don't like to talk about myself too much and always hold feelings pretty close, but I couldn't internalize this. I ended up talking about the situation to close colleagues and friends. That helped me initially.

As time went on, I chose to not put my whole self into my job. I started exercising more, taking yoga classes. I stopped working such long hours and found moments of peace outside the office. I came to see that our whole team had had negative experiences with this manager, and I built a team of support around me. My friends and family were also supportive but asked, "Why are you even still there?" They just didn't get the context—I didn't like this manager, but I loved my job.

When you're getting ready to leave your job, aim high.

I regained some confidence and came to understand that my manager was creating a toxic environment. I thought maybe I should apply to some other companies and see what happened. I was already feeling rejected; if these companies rejected me too, so what? I felt like things couldn't get worse.

If you had asked me, "Where would you want to work if you could work anywhere?" I would have said, "Google." I'd heard that Google had a supportive, inclusive, employee-centric culture, in the sense of "We care about you as a person, your career, your health, your overall life." I also knew I could continue building my marketing career there.

A marketing position opened up in the New York office and I applied for it, thinking I would never hear back. But I got an e-mail from the recruiter, saying, "We looked over your résumé, we'd love to have an intro conversation with you." We talked, and a week later, she called. She had loved our conversation, but my experience wasn't a good fit for the job. She said she would put me at the top of Google's database of marketing applicants, and if a more appropriate position popped up, she'd let me know.

She let me down in the nicest way, I thought as I got off the phone. *I will never hear from her again.*

Three months later, I got an e-mail from a different recruiter within Google. They had a partner marketing position open. The recruiter said, "The only caveat is that it's based in Mountain View," which is Google's headquarters in California.

I had grown up in New Jersey and always lived there. I was such a Jersey girl that the idea of moving anywhere beyond New York seemed crazy. Reflecting on my current situation, I thought, *Rejection isn't going to hurt me. Worst case, I gain some interview experience.* And I started to go through the interview process. There were several interview stages; then I was flown out to California for the last round of in-person interviews.

Within a month I heard back. I actually got the position and decided to take it.

The very first time I talked to my current manager at Google, he said, "Tell me about yourself. Where are you from? What do you like? What's your communication style? How do you like to work with your manager?" It wasn't about my experience, my expertise, my "value-add." He was getting to know me as a person. Just having those initial conversations shed new light on what a manager–direct report relationship could and should be.

In addition to regular check-ins, we have personal development plans, goals for the next few months and the whole year. I get to share my growth priorities—whether I would like more exposure to leadership or to other new challenges or to do more travel. We've recently had a few team members leave our team to join other Google teams, and my manager was so supportive, helping them make the career changes that best suited their goals. He put aside the fact that he needed to find new people to fill the roles. He truly cares about each of us individually and how he can help grow our careers as opposed to just looking at the short term—what we're achieving by the end of the week, for example.

Sometimes I wake up and can't believe that I now live in San Francisco. I can't believe how things have turned around. I just hope that those who are going through similar situations, internalizing rejections at the office, can realize that they're so much more than their particular work situation. It's hard to realize when you're in it, but it helps to arm yourself with support. Then you'll have people in your court, cheering you on.

MARISSA HABY'S TIPS

TIP 1—I remained close with one of my original bosses at Philips, even after he left the company. Just being able to call him and ask, "What do I do? What advice do you have for me?" was helpful. Find advocates and advisors who have more overall career experience, and stay in touch.

TIP 2—It's important to celebrate even those moments that aren't Instagram-worthy. Try to feel good about small accomplishments, even if you are the only one who sees them.

TIP 3—Know your self-worth. It's easy to say and difficult to do, but be kind to yourself.

MARIA KLAWE

The easiest way to get me to do anything is to tell me I shouldn't do it.

As the first female president of Harvey Mudd College, computer scientist and scholar Maria Klawe made it a priority to recruit women and people of color to math, science, and engineering. Harvey Mudd is a private science and engineering college near Los Angeles, and Klawe drew on resources near and far to recruit more women and people of color to the faculty and student body. In computer science, the new faculty led a redesign of courses, so that in addition to learning theoretical concepts in introductory classes, students could apply their knowledge to real-world situations from the start. The computer science faculty also increased opportunities for female students to do research with their professors and took them to conferences in order to network and meet potential mentors. As a result, the number of female computer science majors increased dramatically, and within five years, the numbers of female and male students graduating in computer science were nearly equal. Over the next few years similar changes happened in other departments, and now the number of males and females is roughly equal in all areas of STEM (Science, Technology, Engineering, and Math) at Harvey Mudd. In addition, the number of students of color has increased significantly in all areas.

Klawe came to Harvey Mudd from Princeton, where she was the dean of engineering and professor of computer science. She holds seventeen honorary doctorates and, as a researcher in discrete mathematics and computer science, has made important research contributions. She gives talks all around the world on how to attract and retain women and people of color in STEM fields. In 2014, she was listed as number seventeen on *Fortune* magazine's list of World's 50 Greatest Leaders.

Klawe is also a watercolor artist and did our interview over the phone while she was working on a painting. She is well-known for painting in board meetings.

Lessons I've Learned

Talk about your goals with colleagues. They may have surprising and useful suggestions about how to reach those goals.

I think I'm a lot like my father, who took leaps of faith and action without a safety net. He was born in Poland and joined the resistance against the Nazis; he was arrested but escaped from a concentration camp, journeying through the mountains in Eastern Europe in the middle of winter. Some of his fellow travelers died. He then fought with the free French armies, was wounded, and for some reason evacuated to Scotland. That's where he met my Scottish mother, and they moved to Canada, where they had me and my sisters.

I grew up in Alberta, loving math and science, but when I went to college at the University of Alberta, the whole world was in flux and I got involved in radical student politics. In 1968, after my freshman year, I traveled to Yale and then Berkeley and got arrested as part of the People's Park protest. My parents, who thought I was in Montreal, got a phone call from the Alameda County Sheriff's Office telling them I was in jail. They bailed me out but gave me an ultimatum: "Either stop the radical student politics or we have to disown you," they said. "We think you're destroying your life and you're setting a bad example for your younger sisters." So I walked out, just before I turned eighteen.

I continued going to college, supporting myself, but dropped out junior year. In all my conversations about how to change the world, I couldn't see any way that pure mathematics would make a difference. I moved to the United States to be with a boyfriend I'd met when visiting Yale, and we lived in Buffalo, New York, while he earned money working at a steel mill. Then we traveled to India, essentially overland except for our flight across the Atlantic Ocean.

During that time, I read recreational math books and played chess even though I don't like it. I started to realize that I needed math. I missed it desperately. It was just so clear that I had to use that part of my brain and couldn't live without math being a part of who I was.

From the beaches of Goa, I wrote to my professors in the math department at the University of Alberta. "I want to come back and go straight into my PhD," I said. "I've discovered I have to be a mathematician."

They were very generous and wrote back, saying, "Well, you actually have to finish your undergraduate degree first, but we'll let you finish it in two semesters taking graduate-level classes."

I'd been away from math for almost two years, and now I was going to do graduate-level courses without most of the prerequisites. I worked harder than I ever had in my life, and it completely changed my attitude toward learning, because for the first time, it wasn't easy.

I then went into the PhD program, finished it in four years, and started looking for a job as a professor. At that time, about a thousand people were applying for pure math academic positions, and there were maybe twenty tenure-track positions open in all of the United States and Canada. I got one interview. Although I had known there were very few jobs, I had been confident I'd get the kind of work I wanted, at a university where I could do and teach pure mathematics.

I had a number of postdoc offers but only one tenure-track offer, from Oakland University in Michigan, and with the encouragement of my PhD advisor, I took it. I didn't enjoy it at all, mostly because I was very lonely socially. Another factor was the challenge of teaching topics like multivariable calculus to students who had difficulty adding fractions. This was not what I had planned as a career.

That was the rejection that changed my life, not being hired as a faculty member in a top math department right after my PhD. If I had been hired by a university with strong students I wouldn't have made the changes that I made next, which led me down a completely different path.

Because I was so lonely, I went to conferences as a way of

having people to talk to. By chance, I learned that there were people who did the kind of math I did but in computer science departments. They were getting job offers from places like Harvard and MIT and Bell Labs. When I complained to a colleague that this was unfair, his response was, "Well, go get a second PhD."

He told me about a theoretical physicist who had done this recently and that the best places to get a PhD in theoretical computer science were Stanford, MIT, and the University of Toronto in Canada. Stanford had just closed their admissions process when I called; MIT already had their class of eleven. (Today it would be more like 250.) But the admissions person at the University of Toronto said, "Oh my goodness, you're Canadian! We'd love to have you!" It turned out that the university had funding specifically for Canadians and permanent residents.

In a field where people need you, there will be all kinds of opportunities.

I enrolled as a graduate student at the University of Toronto in computer science without having taken a single computer science course. Given my experience starting mathematics graduate courses after being away from math for almost two years, I figured I could do it with computer science. It was a ton of work, but I did well. Within five months I was getting invitations to apply for computer science faculty positions and ended up being hired by the University of Toronto as a regular faculty member after nine months (I never finished that second PhD). One of my responsibilities was to run a seminar to which I invited computer scientists from around the world as lecturers.

The second lecturer was Nick Pippenger from IBM Research. Nick was one of the shyest people I had ever met, but also the sweetest, most open, extraordinary person. We were very different: I was an outdoorsy person; Nick was not. I was pretty social; Nick was not. But I had been through a bad, abusive relationship and was more interested in whether we shared fundamental priorities. I was twenty-eight and he was thirty-two when we met, and our very first discussions were all about "What's important to you in life? And what are your values?" Within ten days of meeting we were having conversations like "Well, if you were to get married, would you be interested in having children? Are you willing to work in Canada or the US?" Within four weeks of meeting each other, we were engaged to be married, and now we have been married for forty years.

The University of Toronto had been trying to recruit Nick for some time, but IBM Research—where Nick worked—was now also offering me a job. I thought it would make sense to join IBM because Nick could be in an environment where he was comfortable and I could focus on building my research career as a theoretical computer scientist. I had always loved California, and the opportunity to go there seemed wonderful, so we went to be part of a new group in San Jose on theoretical computer science.

At IBM, I deliberately pursued becoming a manager and starting my own research group because I realized I needed to be in a leadership role in order to be a change agent. I was willing to challenge everything, but I always understood the values of the organization, so I was able to couch what I wanted in terms of those values. For example, IBM was one of the top environments for theoretical computer scientists and wanted to stay on top. At the same time, there was this belief that your manager should decide what you work on. For people working at the forefront of a discipline, that doesn't make sense. I argued that to stay ahead, we needed to be more like an academic environment, where researchers have autonomy and control over their projects.

Going to IBM turned out to be amazingly good for my career as an academic leader because they had such good management training. In 1988, when an opportunity came to help build a world-class computer science department at the University of British Columbia, we moved to Vancouver. Our children were six and three and I wanted them to attend public schools in French immersion. Moreover, my parents lived in British Columbia and were getting older. My experiences at UBC took my long-term interest in promoting women in STEM fields to a new level. I was the first female professor in the computer science department, the first female head of a science department, the eleventh female faculty member in science out of about three hundred, and the fourth female full professor out of more than two hundred. When I arrived the university didn't see the small number of female faculty in science as something that needed to be addressed. Over my fourteen and a half years there, I worked hard on this issue, becoming the first female vice president and then the first female dean of science. During my four years as dean of science, we doubled the number of female faculty in science from twenty-four to forty-eight. I also, concurrently with being VP and dean, was the first NSERC Chair for Women in Science and Engineering for British Columbia and the Yukon. During that time we increased the percentage of computer science majors who were female from seventeen percent to twenty-seven percent over five years, joining Carnegie Mellon as the first two universities to address this issue.

Eventually I realized that to have more impact on increasing the participation of women in STEM fields, I would need to return to the United States, and I became the dean of engineering at Princeton. In my third year there I was invited to apply to be president of Harvey Mudd College.

I told Harvey Mudd's search committee that I was not interested and tried to withdraw from the search many times. They kept telling me, "We know you're not interested in the position, but we just like having you as one of our candidates," which apparently is something consultants will do. At a certain point, I became a finalist but was still not planning on going, and I told a close colleague at Princeton about my candidacy. "Why would you ever consider doing that?" she said. "You're supposed to be president of a top research university like Yale or Michigan or Harvard!"

I said to her, "Well, I'm passionate about changing the culture of science and engineering, and I think in many ways it's more set at the undergraduate level than at the graduate level." Still, I was convinced I was going to stay at Princeton.

When Harvey Mudd offered me the presidency, I asked if I could have three weeks to think about it. We were going to be in British Columbia for Christmas vacation, which would allow me space and time. We were on Pender Island for two days before the phone call was going to happen—the one where I'd give them my decision—and the entire time I thought I was staying at Princeton. Just before the call, it was drizzling, and I was looking out at the ocean. The clouds parted and a shaft of light hit the water and I went, "Oh my goodness, I'm about to miss one of the most magical, wonderful opportunities in my life." This kind of thunderbolt realization has never happened to me before, and it's never happened since. But I took the job as president of Harvey Mudd and I've never looked back.

MARIA KLAWE'S TIPS

TIP 1—Be open to new opportunities, especially when they are unexpected. I met Nick on the day I had sworn off dating men forever. I ended up at Harvey Mudd, never expecting to accept the offer.

TIP 2—Hard work and persistence are the most important factors for success. If your goal is ambitious, you will encounter many challenges and seeming failures along the way. Do not give up, but be willing to consider different approaches and strategies.

TIP 3—Ask for help and give help. No single person changes the world by themselves. Find others with similar goals and connect your networks.

PAMELA SHIFMAN

A rejection can mean that something was actually not a good fit. It's worthwhile to do some reflection about whether the thing you thought you wanted was something you *actually* wanted.

It feels like we're in a moment where women's power is unprecedented," Pamela Shifman told me. "I feel hopeful." Getting off the phone with Pamela, I felt hopeful too. She has spent her whole career fighting for the rights of women and girls around the world, most recently at the NoVo Foundation, "resourcing feminist movements all over the world, learning so much, looking at what has been accomplished and where we have to go." By the time she left, NoVo had become one of the largest private foundations in the world explicitly focused on the rights of women and girls.

Movements led by women, Pamela said, are challenging the rise of authoritarianism and populism here and all over the world. She was thinking of Black Lives Matter, founded by three powerful black feminists (Alicia Garza, Patrisse Khan-Cullors, and Opal Tometi), as well as the rising power of social movements, from Brazil and Hungary to Chile, India, and the United States, often led by feminists challenging religious and political extremism, and the influx of progressive women running for political office. "I feel excited," Shifman said, "about the rising power of women, and particularly women of color, low-income women, and other marginalized women who are leading transformative work. I think that is going to shift everything."

Pamela is widely known as a visionary philanthropic leader with an approach that centers those impacted by injustice as experts of their own lives. In her role at the NoVo Foundation, she created groundbreaking initiatives like the Move to End Violence, a decade-long initiative to end violence against women and girls in the United States, and the Collective Future Fund, which invests in women of color fighting gender-based violence. Pamela also led the NoVo Foundation in launching a historic 90-million-dollar commitment to support girls of color in the United States.

Lessons I've Learned

Sometimes we want the things we think we're supposed to want.

I've known since I was young that my life would be dedicated to advancing the rights of women and girls and to ending gender-based violence. I knew people who experienced violence in the home and sexual abuse, and I was acutely aware of gender inequality around me.

In high school, a good friend of mine was stalked by her boyfriend. I didn't have the language to describe it; I just knew he was controlling. After we went to college, my friend survived a terrible attack—the boyfriend ended up traveling to her campus and shooting her in the back of the head at close range, then killing himself. Incredibly, my friend lived. From that point forward, I was clear that my life's work would be about working toward a world in which women can live in safety and dignity.

I was an activist in college and decided to go to law school, not because I wanted to be a lawyer but because I thought it would help me to do social justice policy and advocacy work. In my last year at University of Michigan Law School, I applied for judicial clerkships. It's very common at an elite law school to do a clerkship for two years if you're not going to work for a firm. I applied for at least a hundred clerkships all over the country; then I waited. Letter after letter arrived with first lines like this: "Thank you for your application. You are really wonderful, but we have many wonderful applicants . . ." There were so many rejections that I lost track. I got three interviews but no clerkships. And I was devastated. It felt horrible. I was one of the few people I knew who didn't get a single clerkship offer, and I wondered, *What's wrong with me?*

Law school was ending, and almost all my peers had jobs. If they were going the corporate track, they had offers at firms; if they were doing public interest law, they had fellowships. I was close with a dean of the law school, who ran an international fellowship program where you could make your own project working outside the United States. She encouraged me to apply.

I took the application from her, and as I completed it, I thought for perhaps the first time about what being a judicial law clerk would have meant. A clerk's role is to write the judge's opinions, and the practice is supposed to then make you a better lawyer. In my rush to apply for clerkships, I'd forgotten that I didn't *want* to be a lawyer. A clerkship was prestigious and had seemed like what I was supposed to do but was something I probably wouldn't have liked.

I ended up getting the international fellowship to do a project in South Africa, and it was the best thing I have ever done. I worked in the first democratically elected parliament of South Africa, serving as a legal advisor to the African National Congress Parliamentary Women's Caucus. The women I worked for are still my mentors to this day. They taught me that radical social change is possible and what it takes to get there. They transformed everything about how I saw the world and my career path. I had been focused on racial, gender, and economic justice in the United States, but after two years, I moved back to the United States and ended up pursuing a career dedicated to social justice, especially girls and their rights, globally.

I first worked at Open Society Foundations, then became co–executive director of Equality Now, an international women's rights organization. I worked at the UN for six years, running their work on gender-based violence in conflict-affected settings. Then I went to the NoVo Foundation, which was started in 2006 by Jennifer and Peter Buffett and is dedicated to creating a more just and balanced world. I developed strategies specifically around women and girls, and after six years I became the foundation's executive director. I hired a team to think about how to make the kind of change that we wanted to make in the world. What did that require, and so what did the funding strategy look like?

Behind the rejections are real people, and it's a good idea to acknowledge their humanity.

Grant seekers would contact us to see whether the foundation could support their organizations. There's so much need in the world, and so many people doing powerful, transformative work. But although NoVo had a lot of resources, we had a small staff and could not fund all the excellent work presented to us. I had to tell people no all the time.

Saying no feels really hard, and it took time for me to do it well. I learned not to avoid it because it was uncomfortable; I learned to just say "no" and not "maybe," to not give false hope. It's a cliché that in a romantic breakup, one person says, "It's not you; it's me"—but that was true a lot. Often, there would be incredible work that just wasn't aligned with our strategic goals. The grant seeker's work was going to be perfect for somebody else to fund, but it wasn't perfect for us. Internally at NoVo, we also had to view a no as creating the opportunity for us to say yes when another organization's work came along that was more aligned with our approach.

We took seriously that people put a lot of heart and time and thought into asking for money, and we wanted to put care into responding to their requests. We wanted grant seekers to feel that we'd actually taken the time to see their work. I always reminded myself and the NoVo staff that our no was going to be terrible news for somebody; I didn't want to ever forget that. And if we said no, we tried to have a yes about something else, meaning another way we could help, like an idea about a funder who might be a better fit, or a connection to a like-minded organization.

I will never forget the people who would write and say, "Thank you. That was not the answer I wanted, but I really appreciate what you shared." When people responded in a way that recognized we were doing our best, it helped so much.

After twelve years at the NoVo Foundation, I left, deeply proud of all we had accomplished. In the future I will continue to work to advance the rights of women and girls. That is fundamental to who I am. The status of women and girls, particularly those who are most marginalized, is central to any kind of social change. And I'm very clear that the feminist movements are the ones that are going to bring everyone toward justice.

PAMELA SHIFMAN'S TIPS

TIP 1—When you get a rejection for anything, write back and say, "Thank you for sharing this news. I appreciate you reaching out." You would be surprised how few people acknowledge the person on the other side of the e-mail or phone, and it makes a difference for people to recognize that you're in a relationship with each other—it's not a machine saying no.

TIP 2—It can be easy to do the things that we think we're supposed to do or to want. I think when we do the things that fuel our spirit, when we pursue what we love and are good at, then rejection might come a little less often.

PART 5

Rejection Workbook

Since my last book came out, I've talked to women all over the country about how to cope with mistakes at work, sometimes leading them through steps for building resilience. At the same time, I've continued my job with Smith's wonderful undergraduate students, engaging them in exercises about finding meaning in what they're doing. Then I started working on this book, learning about the research on rejection. As I did, I realized that some of the exercises I've led could help people to develop useful mindsets for coping with rejection.

A few of these were created with colleagues. When I started at Smith, I worked closely with Maureen A. Mahoney, dean of the college emerita, and Jennifer L. Walters, who is now dean of the college at Bryn Mawr. My colleague Rachel Simmons introduced me to the theory of "self-compassion," which is so useful in this context.

All the work I do at Smith is in groups, and it might be particularly gratifying to go through the following exercises with a trusted friend or two. My colleague Jennifer always says, "A story needs a listener," and in a way these exercises help you to generate new stories about yourself. It can feel good to share these. Plus, nearly every person with whom I spoke talked about getting support. Keri Smith talked about her husband and his wise words about haters on the internet: "You don't even know those people." Kate Manne told me about discussing her rejections with her therapist. Chelsea Sunday Kline, who ran for state senate, told me about bombing her first debate but then getting encouragement from her campaign, along with professional training.

All this is to say—when I think of you, the reader, going through these exercises, I hope you will join with others if it feels useful, work on your own if it doesn't, and skip around as you see fit. You can read through what follows to get a sense of it before starting, or just jump in.

Psychologist Dan McAdams has written that each of us builds an identity made of stories, and that those stories evolve and change. Keep what you write in your journal *or* find a place to post it, reminding yourself that your story is always evolving.

EXERCISE 1

Craft a Reminder That
You Are Complex

Actress Alysia Reiner, of *Orange Is the New Black*, goes on auditions all the time and told me that she could make herself crazy waiting around for callbacks, but instead she gets creative and politically involved. She writes and produces her own movies; she is deeply involved in community activism; she is the mother of a daughter. Reiner is doing what Duke University professor Patricia Linville might see as nourishing "self-complexity."

Linville has shown that our self-concept—the way we think about our multiple identities—affects the way we cope with stressful events in our lives. She developed the theory of "self-complexity," which is the phenomenon of having more than one "self-aspect," or definition of ourselves. Higher self-complexity protects us, making it less likely that we will become depressed or otherwise debilitated by disappointment.

Why?

First, when something bad happens, we are able to say, "This is about *one* part of my life; there are others about which I still feel pretty good." Even if we're feeling disheartened about one area (a job, for example), we can still feel good about other areas (friendships, sports achievements, creative projects). The more distinct these pieces of our identity are, the better: It means there is "less spillover" from the bad to the good.

I found the poem below long before I saw Linville's research. I think writing your own version of "Things You Didn't Put on Your Résumé" is a great way to think about self-complexity.

Try this when you're facing (or preparing for) your next risk/possible rejection:

Step 1: Take out a notebook or a piece of paper and a writing utensil.

Step 2: Read this poem by the poet Joyce Sutphen, from her book *Carrying Water to the Field*:

THINGS YOU DIDN'T PUT ON YOUR RÉSUMÉ

How often you got up in the middle of the night
when one of your children had a bad dream,
and sometimes you woke because you thought
you heard a cry but they were all sleeping,
so you stood in the moonlight just listening
to their breathing, and you didn't mention
that you were an expert at putting toothpaste
on tiny toothbrushes and bending down to wiggle
the toothbrush ten times on each tooth while
you sang the words to songs from Annie, *and*
who would suspect that you know the fingerings
to the songs in the first four books of the Suzuki

Violin Method and that you can do the voices
of Pooh and Piglet especially well, though
your absolute favorite thing to read out loud is
Bedtime for Frances *and that you picked*
up your way of reading it from Glynnis Johns,
and it is, now that you think of it, rather impressive
that you read all of Narnia and all of the Ring Trilogy
(and others too many to mention here) to them
before they went to bed and on the way out to
Yellowstone, which is another thing you don't put
on the résumé: how you took them to the ocean
and the mountains and brought them safely home.

Step 3: At the top of a page, write "Things You Didn't Put on Your Résumé" or "Things You Didn't Put on Your Medical School Application" or "Things You Didn't Put on Your LinkedIn."

Step 4: Then write a list, or a poem, or a paragraph, keeping in mind experiences that are unique to you. Some questions to use as prompts are: How do you show your friends that you care about them? What do you know how to make with your hands? When is the last time that you did something unproductive but fun? What is your relationship to the outdoors? To a plant or pet?

Step 5: Post this in a place where you can be reminded of your identities outside work.

EXERCISE 2

Take a Shortcut to Change
Your Perspective

Dr. Elizabeth Bell started down the path to medical school by thinking: *Why don't I encourage myself in the same way I encourage my high school students?* It turns out that using your inner voice to speak encouragingly *to* yourself—or to write *about* yourself—can have a surprising impact on your resilience.

In Ethan Kross's lab at the University of Michigan, researchers study the kinds of experiences that lead people to perseverate and ruminate about rejection. "We know that's harmful," said Dr. Kross, "so one of our questions is: How do we get people to stop?" Kross's research shows that it helps to get distance from the experience, which might seem intuitive; the surprising part is what he's learned about *how* to get distance.

"Imagine that a friend comes to you after a rejection," Kross said. "You'd say, 'You got one rejection. You've got to move on. There will be plenty of other opportunities for you.'" He's found that it helps when people think about themselves in the same friendly way and talk to themselves with non-first-person pronouns.

So rather than thinking, *I was rejected, I must suck,* you

literally use your own name—"Jessica, you don't suck," or other pronouns like "she," "he," "they": "She doesn't suck"—to talk to or about yourself. If you do this internally or in writing, it can kind of trick your brain into objective and rational thinking.

Dr. Kross explained that his method is called "distanced self-talk" and said there's evidence that it does help people cope with rejection.

The exercise that follows has always been a favorite of my students. It's based on Beverly Rollwagen's book in which *every poem* starts with the words "She just wants." I love the whole book but am including two of the poems here so that you can use them as a model.

Step 1: Take out a piece of paper or a notebook and a pen or pencil.

Step 2: Read the following poems by Beverly Rollwagen, from her excellent book *She Just Wants*.

ESSENTIAL

She just wants to keep her essential
sorrow. Everyone wants her to
be happy all the time, but she doesn't
want that for them. There is value in
the thread of sadness in each person.
The sobbing child on an airplane, the
unhappy woman waiting by the phone,
a man staring out the window past his

wife. A violin plays through all of them,
one long note held at the beginning and
the end.

EMPLOYED

She just wants to be employed
for eight hours a day. She is not
interested in a career; she wants a job
with a paycheck and free parking. She
does not want to carry a briefcase filled
with important papers to read after
dinner; she does not want to return
phone calls. When she gets home, she
wants to kick off her shoes and waltz
around her kitchen singing, "I am a piece
of work."

Step 3: Write a couple of paragraphs that begin with the words "She just wants." (Use your pronoun of choice.) If you feel like it, you can make them poems.

Step 4: Think about a rejection that's bothering you. Write a "She just wants" poem or paragraph with that rejection in mind. It's also interesting to try writing in the second person, to a "you."

Step 5: Notice whether doing this exercise brought up new feelings or thoughts about the rejection.

EXERCISE 3
Practice Self-Compassion

Many of the women in this book talked about the impor-tance of feeling your feelings. Comedy Central vice president Tara Schuster told me that instead of resisting the hurt of rejection, she imagined a parent kissing a child's skinned knee. In this scenario, she's the parent *and* the kid with the skinned knee.

Schuster's intuition about how to feel better is resonant with Kristin Neff's research. Perhaps you are familiar with Dr. Neff's theory of self-compassion. Her TED Talk about it has been viewed about one and a half million times. Neff is a psychologist at the University of Texas at Austin who has shown how useful it can be to develop a practice of self-compassion.

It has three main elements.

First, self-compassion includes the mindfulness practice of "be here now"—as in "I was rejected at work and this sucks." You acknowledge what's going on and how you feel about it.

Second, it involves talking to yourself like you would to a close friend instead of beating yourself up. Would you discourage a friend by saying, "Oh, you'll *never* get a job"? Nope. You'd say something comforting and send a funny GIF, or bake them cookies, or invite them out dancing, or to join you for a Netflix binge.

Third, self-compassion means seeing your experience as

connecting you with others, so rather than telling yourself, *I must be the only idiot who's ever dealt with something this bad,* you think, *I guess people go through this. When you're applying for a job, it can suck. This is a universal experience.*

Dr. Neff has published books on self-compassion, including a workbook, and it's worth it to investigate. My friend Susie, a psychotherapist, highlighted for me Neff's concept of "backdraft" because Susie sees this in her patients: When firefighters are trying to put out a fire but open a door and expose the fire to oxygen, the fire flares up—that's called "backdraft." Self-compassion can feel like you are exposing your psyche to oxygen; painful feelings can come rushing out. It can almost feel easier to tamp down the painful feelings by saying mean things to yourself, like "You didn't try hard enough." Neff's research demonstrates that those instincts really don't help.

Self-compassion is different from self-esteem, which well-known psychologist Jean Twenge argues is *not* associated with emotional well-being, and in fact, Twenge believes, has more to do with narcissism. So having self-compassion is less about how you see yourself and more about developing a research-informed approach to coping when things go wrong. Of course, like all that is worth doing, this approach requires practice. Here are some steps to begin.

Step 1: If possible, watch one of Kristin Neff's talks online.

Step 2: Go through the three steps of self-compassion: Acknowledge how you feel about the rejection that you're dealing with; then say something to yourself that you would say to a close friend; then think about how this bad experience actually *connects* you to others who go through similar things.

Step 3: Practice self-compassion whenever you can, and investigate Neff's website. She has lots of free resources online that will allow you to go deeper.

Exercise 4

Practice Growth Mindset through Sketching "Photos" You Didn't Take

When she was working at JPMorgan, Isa Watson got feedback that felt vague. She needed to work on her "analytics." What did that mean? Watson told me, "They meant I wasn't strong at building models and analyzing business data. Mind you, I had a degree in economics from MIT with a concentration in financial engineering (graduating with honors). I had more analytics skills than anyone around me—and their opinion on it had nothing to do with my skill, but with their biases." Indeed, black women often face prejudice at work and are less likely than their white colleagues to be supported by managers.

This means black women are also less likely to get useful critiques. Business school researcher Robin Ely, who studies gender at work, told me that women of color and white women are more likely to get vague, positive feedback than information on how to improve. "When men fail, in general they get more feedback and can learn from it," she said. "When women fail, we often don't even know what happened and kind of have to figure things out ourselves."

Why? Ely reminded me that it's hard to give feedback at all and told me about "benevolent sexism." This can go hand in hand with benevolent racism. Supervisors don't want to discourage women and people of color, but their "kindness" actually ends up hurting.

This is a good reminder to ask supervisors, "Would you tell me *one* area in which you think I could improve?" Ask for detailed information.

And then—if that detailed information makes you feel crappy, which of course it temporarily could—remember Stanford professor Carol Dweck's theory of "growth mindset." Dweck teaches people that the brain changes with learning and that practice on a task enhances your skill at that task. An important part of her theory is that people who *believe* their skills will improve through focused practice are more likely to actually improve.

It would be wrong to think of growth mindset as a mandate to "just persevere." It's more about *how* we do that and the way in which we *think about* what we're doing. That's why the following exercise invites you to get very specific about the way in which you've worked to learn something.

Step 1: Take out a piece of paper and a pen or pencil; for this exercise, you could also grab some colored pencils or markers.

Step 2: Write down one thing in your life you thought you weren't good at or were afraid to try, but you practiced and got better at it. This could be riding a bike, baking bread, doing spreadsheets, parenting a toddler, or really anything else!

Step 3: Draw three empty boxes for your three imaginary photos.

Step 4: Try to look back at the thing you chose and remember important moments in practicing each thing. If you could take a photo of each moment, what would that photo look like? For example, with "baking bread," I might include a (sketched) "photo" of me standing in front of my oven, surrounded by broken glass. I had put a Pyrex pan of water in the oven to "steam" bread—as per a reader comment in an online recipe—and the Pyrex exploded all over my kitchen.

Step 5: Draw three NEW boxes. Now instead of thinking back on a skill that you learned, think ahead to a skill that you WANT to learn. How might you practice in order to improve? What might some of the steps be? Sketch or write them in each of the three empty boxes.

Step 6: Post both sketches—the thing you already learned and the thing you are *going to learn*—somewhere you can see them.

Step 7: Based on your sketches, what are some of the steps for learning what you want to learn? Choose one step to work on. Then begin a "one-sentence diary" to chart your progress—add a single sentence every day about something you've done to work toward getting better at that particular step.

EXERCISE 5
Reflect on Purpose

from Educator and Consultant Lara Galinsky

Having a sense of purpose can help you get past rejection. Psychologist Angela Duckworth's graduate school advisor said her research wouldn't work, but she realized she didn't need his permission and went ahead with it. It led to a breakthrough that propelled her early career.

My friend Lara Galinsky has been thinking about "purpose" for more than a decade and has developed some of my favorite exercises to help people reflect on and find purpose. She now works with individuals, nonprofits, and companies as a consultant, and the work always centers on purpose. I like her definition, which she adapts from the work of researchers William Damon, Kendall Cotton Bronk, and Jenni Menon Mariano: "Purpose is a stable and generalized intention to accomplish something that is at the same time meaningful to the self and consequential for the world beyond the self."

Lara begins by raising some myths about purpose. These include the idea that purpose is fixed; in fact, it can change throughout your life as you learn, grow, and mature as a person. It's a myth that purpose has to align with your career perfectly, like a bull's-eye. It can, Lara says, but doesn't have to. Purpose can be fulfilled through your family life or hobbies, or even the way you treat people each and every day. It's a myth that purpose is a luxury; a major study recently found that having a sense of purpose contributed to living longer! In addition to basic needs, Lara says everyone deserves to have a sense of purpose.

In "The Genuine," the consulting workbook that she developed for use with clients, Lara guides people through a process of reflecting on purpose within themselves. I was excited that she let me include some of her questions below. In her model, she specifies purpose *within* (your virtues, values, and qualities) and purpose *beyond* (your contribution to your family, community, an issue, a company/organization, or the world). The model is based on taking that which is *within* you into fruition to fulfill what is *beyond* you.

Step 1: Take out a notebook or piece of paper and a writing utensil.

Step 2: Reflect on and write in response to the following questions. Let yourself write without judgment or even editing. See what flows from you as you write.

- What are three to five values that are a key part of who you are?

- What's irreducibly *you*? If we asked people from different parts of your life about you, what are three to five adjectives they would use?

- What roles do you repeatedly play with others or in groups? List three to five descriptors (e.g., organizer, teacher, convener, visionary, disrupter).

- How do you want people to experience your energy? When you leave a space, what do you hope to leave behind?

Then Lara asks these questions about purpose beyond the self:

- What in your family line do you want to carry forward? What do you want to disrupt, change, or heal? List three to five ideas.

- What currently lights you up or brings you into a flow state? List three to five ideas or activities. What patterns can you discern from these?

- Is there something that you return to over and over in your hopes and dreams, something you may have never completed and want to return to?

- What contribution do you want to offer the world? What problem do you feel a drive and responsibility to solve?

Take a look at what you wrote to do some sense-making. Do you see any patterns? Any new connections? Did anything emerge that's surprising to you? Lara often asks people to circle phrases that have "heat"—they contain clues or cues about what's important to you now, even if you might not fully understand their importance.

Again, we think about purpose as singular, saying things like "My purpose in life . . ." or "The purpose of this is . . ." but it's important to recognize that what we are doing can have multiple purposes, and that they can change over time. So if you are dealing with a rejection at work, take time to think about why you are doing the work—what are some of the deeper purposes?

EXERCISE 6

Get Ten "Nos"

from Laura Huang, PhD, Author of *Edge:
Turning Adversity into Advantage*

In order to practice dealing with rejection, Professor Laura Huang advises her students at Harvard Business School to try to get ten people to say no to them. This is a great way to bring a sense of humor to risk taking, to practice dealing with rejection—and like Professor Huang's students, you may get some surprising yeses.

The assignment is literally to get ten people to say no. Huang told me that "it can't be a hedge like, 'Oh, I can't do this, but instead I'll do that.' If students get a hedge, they have to start all over again." As each of the ten people says no to them, Huang's students write a short paragraph about the no.

During the process, her students get to interact with a range of people, trying different communication styles and kinds of asks. They also make interesting discoveries. "We're so used to trying to get people to say yes to us, always wanting people to like and agree with us," Huang said. "So when the assignment is to get people to say no to you, it leads you to consider: Who are the people that I'm going to? Who's saying no? How am I communicating? You're

building a different set of muscles, learning about how you're being perceived, how you perceive others."

She said that students also realize people are much more likely
to say yes than you think. "There are some absurd things that
people have gotten from this exercise that they haven't expected
at all," she told me. "One student came back with two Super
Bowl tickets. Another student came back with the promise of a
one-week stay at a person's vacation home."

The "Ten Nos" exercise is one that you can certainly try on
your own but that might be fun to try with a friend or even a
group. Here are the basic steps:

Step 1: Take out a notebook or piece of paper and a writing
utensil.

Step 2: Make a list of things that you could ask for! You can
start small: If you are a student, maybe you ask for an extension
on a paper. If you are a working person, maybe a friend who is
good at taking pictures would do a LinkedIn (or Tinder?) photo
shoot for you. Be creative.

Step 3: Just so you know—each yes doesn't count. You have to
gather ten nos. Make sure that you are keeping track of your state
of mind before you ask, and after. Take notes. Gather data about
ways of asking that seem to work, and about what helps you feel
okay about a no.

EXERCISE 7

Imagine You Are Being
Interviewed for This Book

When I interviewed participants in this book, I asked, "Tell me about the development of your career and about one important work-related rejection." I was interested in a rejection that had served as a touchstone in some way, because they had learned from it, or a rejection that had just stayed with them even if they weren't sure why.

The work of researcher Melissa Peet has informed the way I interview anyone; I teach students about what I learned from Peet and her process of "generative knowledge interviewing." The goal of her technique is to uncover *tacit knowledge,* meaning the stuff you know deep inside but haven't consciously articulated to yourself.

This can be transformative. I remember one student, Kenzi. During a workshop, she described an international journalism internship she'd had, where she was "sent on assignment to meet with Bedouin villagers whose homes were slated to be demolished in the coming months."

But Kenzi didn't want to write about this experience.

Surrounded by her peers in our workshop room at Smith, she pulled me aside and told me she was going to delete what she'd started. She'd never want to disclose the fact that her editor had rejected the article, telling her that news of this demolishment wasn't "new."

As we discussed it, Kenzi realized the rejection wasn't a story to hide. It was indeed a seminal story about how she'd realized she didn't actually want to be a journalist but instead wanted to do international human rights work.

I tell Kenzi's story to show that reflecting deeply on a rejection can be personally useful as a way to demonstrate how you developed your own values and goals. Kenzi actually ended up using what she wrote about this "rejection" to get into graduate school at Oxford, and she now works in foreign policy.

The following is an exercise based on what I did with Kenzi, and what we still do at Smith as we guide students to reflect on what's gone well but also on challenges that inform who they are. You can do this with friends, interviewing one another, or on your own.

Step 1: Get a notebook or piece of paper and writing utensil.

Step 2: Write about an experience of disappointment or rejection—something that didn't go as you had hoped.

The next steps can be done on your own, or you can use them as interview questions.

Step 3: Zoom in on one key moment. Where were you? Who were you with? What was happening? Can you describe it almost like you are describing a scene in a movie?

Step 4: In this moment of disappointment or rejection, what did you do well? (Or what did you learn?)

Step 5: What are the skills and values that are part of who you are that *allowed you* to do something well, or to learn, even during a crappy work moment?

ACKNOWLEDGMENTS

I am most grateful to the women who agreed to participate in this book. You were extremely generous in offering your time, and I learned so much from you. Thank you.

I am also grateful to my colleagues at Smith College. Susan Etheredge, I appreciate the way you worked to create a place for reflection and integration at the college. Borjana Mikic, I have been very lucky to have you as my boss. You're both smart and wise. You're a true leader, and I'm learning from you every day. Erin Cohn, Emily Norton, Monica Dean, René Heavlow, and Stacie Hagenbaugh—I've never been part of such an amazing work team. Thank you for being brilliant and funny and creative and just great colleagues. Stacie, thank you also for your excellent ideas for this book.

Thank you to Lidia Ortiz, Shanice Bailey, and Tiffany Cho, who generously agreed to read through the interviews as I was looking for themes.

I also would like to thank the many friends, family members, and colleagues who helped me find participants for the book: Arielle Eckstut, Jessica Goldstein, Fran Rosenfeld, Ben Berkman, Sarah Moore, Andy Sokatch, and Rachel Simmons.

I want to thank Kate Napolitano, because I learned so much

from you in editing my first book, and you are an important person to me.

Lindsay Edgecombe, my agent, is the smartest and kindest and best agent ever, and I felt fortunate to have the wonderful Jill Schwartzman at Plume as my editor. Jill's support of this book from the beginning kept me going. When I was overwhelmed, an e-mail from Jill always made me feel good. And she is a Smith alumna! I hit the jackpot.

To my parents, Jim and Joan Levine, my brother, Josh Levine, my parents-in-law, Debby and Joel, and my sister-in-law, Gabrielle: I am lucky to have you all in my life!

Finally, I want to thank Edie and Elijah. I love you and am so proud of who you are. Joe Bacal, you are my growth mindset role model, continuously learning new things, and you are the funniest person I know. Thanks for being yourself and for always supporting me.

ABOUT THE AUTHOR

Jessica Bacal is the editor of *Mistakes I Made at Work: 25 Influential Women Reflect on What They Got Out of Getting It Wrong* (Penguin Random House, 2014). She is also director of reflective and integrative practices and of the Narratives Project at Smith College in Northampton, Massachusetts. Before coming to Smith, she taught elementary school in New York City. She received an MSEd in elementary education from Bank Street College, an MFA in creative writing from Hunter College, and an EdD in higher education management from the University of Pennsylvania. She lives with her husband, children, and two dogs.